Elite • 184

World War II Allied Sabotage Devices and Booby Traps

GORDON L. ROTTMAN ILLUSTRATED BY PETER DENNIS

Consultant editor Martin Windrow

First published in Great Britain in 2010 by Osprey Publishing,
Midland House, West Way, Botley, Oxford OX2 0PH, UK
44-02 23rd St, Suite 219, Long Island City, NY 11101

Email: info@ospreypublishing.com

© 2010 Osprey Publishing Ltd.

Print ISBN: 978 184908 175 7
PDF ebook ISBN: 978 1 84908 176 4

Editor: Martin Windrow
Page layout by: Ken Vail Graphic Design, Cambridge, UK (kvgd.com)
Index by Mike Parkin
Typeset in Sabon and Myriad Pro
Originated by PPS Grassmere, Leeds, UK
Printed in China through World Print Ltd

10 11 12 13 14   9 8 7 6 5 4 3 2 1

A CIP catalogue record for this book is available from the British Library

www.ospreypublishing.com

Osprey Publishing is supporting the Woodland Trust, the UK's leading
woodland conservation charity, by funding the dedication of trees.

ACKNOWLEDGMENTS

The author is indebted to Dr Graham Turbinville, William Schneck, William
Howard of the Technical Intelligence Museum, Bruce Hanesalo of
Military/Info Publishing, and David Gordon for allowing the author to
photograph items in his collection.

ARTIST'S NOTE

Readers may care to note that the original paintings from which the colour
plates in this book were prepared are available for private sale. All
reproduction copyright whatsoever is retained by the Publishers. All
enquiries should be addressed to:

Peter Dennis, Fieldhead, The Park, Mansfield, Nottinghamshire NG18 2AT, UK

The Publishers regret that they can enter into no correspondence upon this
matter.

Title page: Wrecked locomotives sabotaged by the French
Resistance in an engine shed at the Annemasse railroad depot.
(IWM ZZZ11837E)

Abbreviations	
AFV	armored fighting vehicle
detcord	detonating cord (aka instantaneous detonating fuse, primacord, cordtex)
OSS	Office of Strategic Services (US organization controlling agents behind enemy lines)
PE	plastic explosive (aka *plastique*)
SOE	Special Operations Executive (British organization controlling agents behind enemy lines)
TNT	trinitrotoluene (high explosive)

METRIC WEIGHT CONVERSION

Metric	English/American
200 grams	7.5oz
300 grams	10.5oz
400 grams	14oz
500 grams	15.5oz
1 kilogram	2.2lb

CONTENTS

WORLD WAR II ALLIED SABOTAGE DEVICES AND BOOBY TRAPS

INTRODUCTION

The US Army's post-World War II field manual FM 5-31, *Boobytraps*, included many techniques and lessons learned from that war. It described a booby trap as "an explosive charge cunningly contrived to be fired by an unsuspecting person who disturbs an apparently harmless object or performs a presumably safe act. Two types are in use – improvised and manufactured.

Posed photo of a member of the French Resistance setting an explosive charge on a railroad line. Unless the charges were going to be detonated immediately they needed to be well concealed to prevent patrols detecting them; this meant they had to be placed beneath the rail, dug into the roadbed's gravel ballast and covered to make the site look natural. Any fuse or firing wires leading off to the side also had to be buried and camouflaged, or they would be easily detectable. Such precautions required at least three times more time than simply emplacing charges against the track – which could be a serious consideration, depending on local security patrols. An additional benefit, however, was that the buried charges generated more explosive power, as the blast was directed upward. (Imperial War Museum HU56936)

Improvised booby traps are assembled from specially provided material or constructed from materials generally used for other purposes. Manufactured booby traps are dirty-trick devices made at a factory for issue to troops. They usually imitate some object or article that has souvenir appeal or that may be used by the target to advantage." Mechanical booby traps date back at least to the American Civil War, seeing limited use in other conflicts thereafter, and gradually wider employment in World War I. (The term "booby trap" dates from about 1850, but as long ago as *c.*1600 a "booby" was defined as an awkward, foolish person.)

In World War II, by the summer of 1940 the British Empire and Commonwealth found itself on the defensive and alone in the war against Germany and Italy. Although Germany's invasion of the USSR in mid-1941 opened another vast front, the situation would only deteriorate further until December 1941, when Japan entered the war on a tide of immediate victories. Even though the United States, "the arsenal of democracy," was simultaneously forced into the world war, the Allies would remain on the defensive for some time. In the meantime Britain, and later the Americans, sought a means, however limited, to strike back and keep the Axis off balance. Among military units, the British Commandos and later the Australian Independent Companies were raised to conduct amphibious raids and guerrilla-type operations. Subsequently, various other British special-mission military units were raised, to include the Special Air Service (SAS), Special Boat Section – later Service (SBS), and in the Middle East the Long-Range Desert Group (LRDG) and "Popski's Private Army" (PPA).[1]

Under the Foreign Office (foreign ministry), Britain already had an effective Secret Intelligence Service ("MI6") to collect, analyze and disseminate intelligence, and, under the Home Office, the Security Service ("MI5"), which performed counterintelligence and countersubversion duties with notable success from the first. However, Prime Minister Churchill also instructed his government to "Set Europe ablaze!" by more direct action, and in parallel with MI6 the Special Operations Executive (SOE) was created. This independent organization was to formulate and execute plans to damage the Axis war effort by unconventional means, including subversion and sabotage. The SOE would supply and support the French *Maquis*, and also resistance and partisan groups in the Netherlands, Belgium, most of Norway, Denmark, Poland, Czechoslovakia, Greece, and Yugoslavia.[2]

In the meantime, America was behind the power curve. Its intelligence services, too, came under different government departments, mainly State

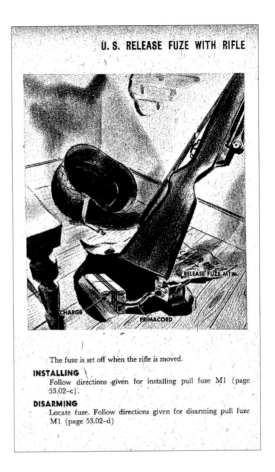

U. S. RELEASE FUZE WITH RIFLE

The fuze is set off when the rifle is moved.

INSTALLING
Follow directions given for installing pull fuze M1 (page 53.02–c).

DISARMING
Locate fuze. Follow directions given for disarming pull fuze M1 (page 53.02–d).

Drawing in a US manual demonstrating how to booby-trap a Garand rifle; a well-trained enemy was not always attracted to souvenir-hunting, but a usable semiautomatic weapon was highly desirable. A hole is shown cut in the floorboards, with the rifle butt resting on a pressure-release device linked to four $\frac{1}{2}$lb TNT blocks, the trap being camouflaged with a sheet of paper. This is not the most convincing means of concealment, and a wary soldier would avoid it and mark it as dangerous. It would be better to place the butt on a light, freely pivoting section of loosened floorboard resting on the pressure plate – but in that case removing the arming pin when setting the trap would be dangerously difficult. Booby-trapping was not a task for the unskilled.

1 See Osprey Elite 64: *Army Commandos 1940–45*; and Battle Orders 23: *Axis and Allied Special Forces 1940–43*
2 See Osprey Warrior 133: *SOE Agent*; and Warrior 117: *French Resistance Fighter*. *Maquis* literally means "brushwood" or "scrub," from the terrain where irregulars traditionally took refuge; more formally, the Resistance was designated from February 1944 the French Forces of the Interior – *Forces Françaises de l'Intérieur.*

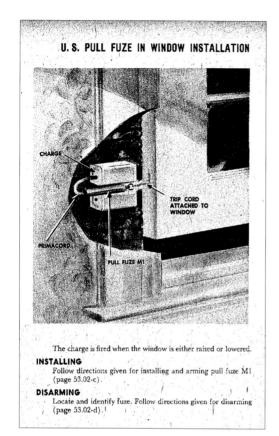

U.S. PULL FUZE IN WINDOW INSTALLATION

CHARGE

PRIMACORD

TRIP CORD ATTACHED TO WINDOW

PULL FUZE M1

The charge is fired when the window is either raised or lowered.

INSTALLING
Follow directions given for installing and arming pull fuze M1 (page 53.02-c).

DISARMING
Locate and identify fuze. Follow directions given for disarming (page 53.02-d).

Hidden inside the framing of a partly open sash window, an M1 pull-firing device is attached to the window and linked by a short length of detcord (instantaneous fuse) to two ½lb TNT blocks. These will detonate when the window is raised or lowered.

and Justice (FBI), and the Army and Navy jealously guarded their own intelligence services. A Coordinator of Information was established in July 1941 under MajGen William J. Donovan, but he had virtually no authority over the existing services. Unable to actually coordinate intelligence activities, "Wild Bill" Donovan's office grew into the Office of Strategic Services (OSS) in June 1942.[3] The OSS was not a national intelligence agency overseeing all US intelligence activities, but was tasked to collect and analyze strategic information required by the Joint Chiefs of Staff, and to conduct special operations not assigned to other agencies. These included espionage, subversion, propaganda, and indirect and direct support of partisan forces in Bulgaria, Romania, Finland, northern Norway, and in China and Burma; in conjunction with the British SOE, the OSS also conducted operations in Western European countries already penetrated by that organization.

Both the SOE and the OSS experienced growing pains. They suffered from infighting, from non-acceptance and obstruction by competing organizations and reluctant conventional commands, and – in the face of effective German counterintelligence efforts – both organizations had to learn lessons the hard way during sometimes costly missions.

MUNITIONS AND MATERIALS

A very wide variety of munitions, materials and devices were employed for sabotaging and booby-trapping Axis targets. Most of these were purpose-made, but standard demolition materials were also used, especially when bulk explosives were needed.[4] Among the standard munitions employed, hand grenades were especially valuable for booby-trapping. Numerous grenade-like "bombs" were also developed for sabotage and other destruction purposes, and much use was made of incendiary devices.

Allied troops did not employ booby traps to the same extent as the Axis.[5] This was mainly because from 1942 the Allies were largely on the offensive, but even when in defense and during pauses in offensive operations the Allies were not particularly noted for their use of booby traps. These are more valuable when forces are in retreat; anything that will slow down and hamper the morale of the advancing enemy is of benefit, and when friendly forces are in retreat there is little concern that their own booby traps will be a threat to them.

However, Allied tactical booby-trapping was not unknown, and one tactic frequently employed in all theaters is exemplified by its use by the US 11th

3 See Elite 173: *Office of Strategic Services 1942–45*. Immediately after World War II the OSS was in the process of being broken up and its activities were being reassigned to other agencies, but in 1947 it was reconstituted and became the CIA.
4 For more details of specific demolition materials, see Elite 160: *World War II Infantry Assault Tactics*.
5 See Elite 100: *World War II Axis Booby Traps and Sabotage Tactics*.

SAFETY AND LEGALITY

Sabotage devices and booby traps are designed to inflict casualties and/or cause material damage. This can apply to the maker, installer, friendly personnel, and innocent individuals as well as the intended victims. The manufacture of the components of these devices, especially explosives and detonators, can be extremely dangerous. Setting up and arming a booby trap can be as dangerous to the person doing it as to the intended victims. **This book is emphatically not a "how to" manual;** the information is intended for historical study only. Readers are implored not to attempt to manufacture any form of sabotage device or booby trap or their components. Those described in this book were fabricated from military-issue munitions and accessories, not homemade expedients; no attempt should be made to manufacture such devices using modern equivalent materials and components.

Laws vary greatly between countries, but for the most part national and local laws prohibit the use of explosive or "infernal" devices – that is, **any** form of unattended device that may cause harm to a person or property, whether or not that person has entered the property legally. The manufacture of such devices, whether explosive or mechanical, can lead to a charge of criminal possession of a weapon or destructive device or of reckless endangerment. In light of today's virtually unrestrained liability suits, it would be **extremely foolish** for a person to construct any form of booby trap, regardless of its intent or the degree of injury it might inflict. Today's greatly heightened security measures have also created an environment in which any form of suspicious device or material, including replicated inert and simulated devices used by re-enactors, can get a person into serious trouble. Use good judgment: anything that looks even remotely like an ordnance device will invoke a strong response by authorities – if confronted by authorities, immediately declare such devices.

Never, under any circumstances, attempt to modify or tamper with any component of any type of live ordnance device.

Airborne Division on Luzon in 1945. Troops sometimes pulled back from defensive positions at night and prepared new positions covering the first, leaving behind them in the old positions booby traps (mainly trip-wired grenades), and ranging the area with mortars and machine guns. If the Japanese discovered that positions were abandoned or they launched one of their common pre-dawn attacks, on charging into the old positions they were greeted by exploding grenades and long-range fire. Another tactic was for combat patrols to infiltrate at night and emplace booby traps and mines on roads and trails leading out of enemy positions, in the hope they would activate them when they sent out their own patrols or moved out. It was actually hoped that the enemy would discover and deactivate any unexploded mines and booby traps remaining after such operations, thus eliminating them as a threat to advancing friendly units.

The most common Allied booby traps involved fitting landmines with antitampering devices that would explode them if an attempt was made to remove them. Trip-wired hand grenades were also frequently used as booby traps, often emplaced in barbed wire obstacles. Early-warning devices were a form of booby trap emplaced in obstacles and on avenues of approach to

A British Mk III "Clam charge." The black plastic case, fitted with magnets at both ends, measures $5\frac{3}{4}$in × $2\frac{3}{4}$in × $1\frac{1}{2}$in, and held 8oz of Tetryl/TNT; it was used to cut railroad tracks and small steel girders, and to destroy vehicle engine blocks. Here a No.9 Mk I "time pencil" delay-firing device is held in its slot compartment by a spring clip, with the labeled safety pin indicating the delay time still in place. Note that the British .303in rifle round included for scale in this and several other photos is 3.1in/78mm long. (David Gordon Collection)

warn of any prowling enemy. Soldiers demonstrated ingenuity in fabricating such devices, as purpose-made examples were not always available.

Development and liaison

Besides standard military munitions, weapons, and equipment, the SOE and OSS developed their own specialized equipment. These included small hand weapons, specialized firearms, long-range radios, encryption equipment, navigation aids, non-explosive and mechanical sabotage devices, special explosive and incendiary charges, chemical sabotage devices, and many more items.

Most such devices needed to be compact, easily concealed, and low cost, requiring little or no care to maintain, being simple to operate by inexperienced civilians, adaptable in use, reliable, and effective. Packaged items were accompanied by instructions printed on light, easy-to-destroy paper in the form of wordless pictographs; some complex-to-operate items were provided with written instructions in up to seven languages, but still they bore no hints of the item's origin.

The OSS had a complex procedure to determine equipment and materiel needs, and to pursue development, production, and distribution. Checks were in place to ensure that developmental items were both necessary and practicable. It was recognized that a great deal of time and resources could be wasted on items that might have sounded like a good idea, but which, despite naïve early enthusiasm, were in truth impractical or simply unnecessary.

Special weapons and equipment under development by the OSS were approved by the Office of Scientific Research and Development (OSRD), and developed by the National Defense Research Committee (NDRC), which was

Bottom and top of a British Mk IV limpet mine; the magnets around its flat surface allowed it to be attached to ships' hulls, bridge girders, etc., under water. The other side shows a ring, by which the mine could be lowered below water level with the collapsible placement rod shown beside it. (David Gordon Collection)

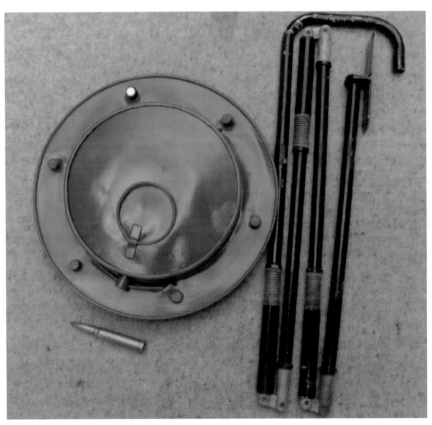

subordinate to the OSRD. The OSRD also coordinated with the armed forces' services of supply, and with the British. The Research and Development Branch had overall responsibility for R&D, coordinated with the OSRD, and NDRC's Division 19, the technical division. This was the Maryland Research Laboratory, where items were made and tested in prototype; if the lab was overworked, projects were farmed out to university and private laboratories and research facilities. Division 19 included a User Trial Committee made up of representatives of the NDRC, British Liaison Mission, Maryland Research Laboratory, and the OSS's Procurement and Supply Branch. The SOE had its own development branch; such liaison prevented the two organizations from developing items with similar capabilities, and allowed them to develop interchangeable items – both special services adopted items developed by the other.

The SOE Inter Service Research Bureau oversaw the development of British equipment, codenamed "Toys," and also tasked other organizations and facilities with R&D. Development of sabotage devices and special equipment was undertaken at a facility at Whitechurch known as The Firs; other sites were an estate called The Frythe (SOE Station IX, in Welwyn Garden City), and Aston House (Station XII).

Sabotage devices, especially explosives and incendiaries, had to be field-tested, not only to prove that they functioned as desired and caused the expected damage, but also to ensure they were safe to transport and handle, remained useable after prolonged storage, were resistant to temperature extremes, water, and rough handling, and were easy to use by untrained individuals under adverse conditions. Even expedient methods of sabotage also had to be tested and verified: for example, just how much sugar was it necessary to introduce into a truck's gas tank to damage the engine?

Explosives

A wide variety of specialized demolition charges and accessories were used, of which only the most commonly employed are discussed here.

Standard-issue demolition charges were available as cylindrical cartridges and slab-like square or rectangular blocks. Sizes varied, but most weighed from a few ounces to under 4lb; smaller charges were protected by paper or cardboard while larger sizes had thin metal covers. Many had one or more threaded fuse wells; plastic explosives did not need fuse wells, as a hole for inserting the detonator could simply be made with a pointed stick or spike. The US and UK usually had standard threading for detonators and other firing devices, making them interchangeable between different types of munitions including mines and grenades, thus allowing these to be used for booby traps. The British developed a specialized shaped-charge munition generally known as "limpet mines." These were fitted with magnets to allow them to be attached to the hulls of ships below the waterline. It would take a number of these charges to actually sink a ship; the hole they created was rather small, and a flooding compartment could easily be sealed by damage-repair crews. However, like any other type of hand-emplaced shaped charges, limpets were also useful for cutting steel beams, rails, pipes, and similar targets.

TNT was among the most commonly used military explosives, and was a component of others. The relative effectiveness of military explosives is rated by their blast effect compared to TNT, which has an effectiveness value of "1." PETN has a value of 1.42, but is too sensitive to shock and flash for military use – it detonates too easily. Amatol (rated at 1.2), tetrytol (1.22),

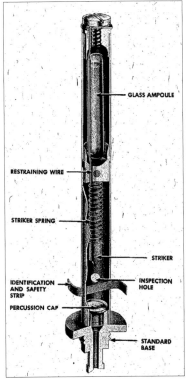

- GLASS AMPOULE
- RESTRAINING WIRE
- STRIKER SPRING
- STRIKER
- IDENTIFICATION AND SAFETY STRIP
- PERCUSSION CAP
- INSPECTION HOLE
- STANDARD BASE

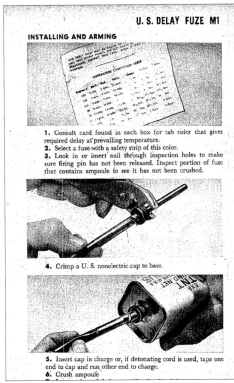

U. S. DELAY FUZE M1

INSTALLING AND ARMING

1. Consult card found in each box for tab color that gives required delay at prevailing temperature.
2. Select a fuze with a safety strip of this color.
3. Look in or insert nail through inspection holes to make sure firing pin has not been released. Inspect portion of fuze that contains ampoule to see it has not been crushed.

4. Crimp a U. S. nonelectric cap to base.

5. Insert cap in charge or, if detonating cord is used, tape one end to cap and run other end to charge.
6. Crush ampoule

LEFT
Designated the M1 delay fuze, British "time pencils" were also used by the American forces, fitted with US fuse adapters. This cutaway drawing shows the glass ampoule of corrosive, the spring-loaded striker, the inspection hole, the identification/safety tab, and the percussion cap.

RIGHT
US manual instructions for using the delay fuze. After consulting the card listing the delays at prevailing temperatures, the user selects a color-coded fuze; checks the inspection hole, and the condition of the top end holding the ampoule; crimps a blasting cap to the fuze; and inserts the cap into the well of a TNT block. Finally he crushes the ampoule, checks the striker once again, and removes the safety tab.

and pentolite (1.26) were more powerful but still stable explosives, widely used in combat demolitions; pentolite was employed in many shaped charges owing to its high detonating velocity.

Plastic explosives (aka Nobel's No.808, *plastique*) were in their infancy in World War II. They were scarce early in the war, but OSS, SOE, and special operations units were given priority because of PE's very useful characteristics and power. PE was composed of RDX (1.60 value) or Hexogen – explosives more powerful than TNT – mixed with plasticizing materials to form a moldable explosive. Early plastic explosives were often oily, had a strong odor, generated unsafe fumes, and became stiff or crumbly at low or high temperature extremes. If the mix was stiff, Vaseline could be kneaded into it to restore its elasticity, but agents who had to work with it complained of headaches and nausea caused by the fumes. Another moldable explosive was gelignite, composed of gun cotton (nitrocellulose) dissolved in nitroglycerine and mixed with wood pulp and potassium nitrate (saltpeter). Unlike PE, this could detonate if struck by a bullet.

The British used a lot of ammonium nitrate-based explosives. Straight ammonium nitrate was a comparatively low-powered explosive, so to make it more effective it was mixed with additives. Alumatol consisted of 70 percent ammonium nitrate, 20 percent TNT, and 3 percent powdered aluminum to protect against moisture.

Accessories

Safety fuse (aka time, delay, or Bickford's fuse) was about 0.25in (6.5mm) in diameter and consisted of a uniform-burning pyrotechnic compound core within a tight, spirally wrapped fiber sheath, with an outer treated-fabric waterproofing cover. The cover of US safety fuse was bright green, and it burned 1ft in 30–45 seconds; British No.11 time fuse was black, and burned 3ft in 20 seconds – a very fast fuse, but not completely waterproof. The burning rate of any given safety fuse could vary between manufacturers' lots, so it needed to be tested before use.

Detonating cord or instantaneous fuse – aka detcord or primacord (US) or cordtex (UK) – was commonly used to link charges to achieve simultaneous detonation. While similar in thickness and appearance to safety fuse, detcord is much different in use and function. Detonating cord is usually covered with a plastic or treated-fabric waterproof covering. The cord is filled with a high-velocity explosive, usually PETN, that detonates at a speed of 21,000 feet per second (6,405 meters per second) – something in the order of 200 miles per minute. It is an explosive charge in its own right. To detonate it, a non-electric blasting cap is taped to an end and a length of safety fuse is inserted in the cap, or an electric blasting cap (detonator) is used, or some form of mechanical firing device is attached. The detcord can be inserted in the fuse wells of demolition charges, with a blasting cap crimped to the end to ensure detonation of the main charge, or alternatively several wraps of detcord are turned around the charge, to link any number of charges. When the detcord is fired it detonates instantaneously, blowing all connected charges simultaneously. US detcord was yellowish-green; the British equivalent was usually covered with lead–or aluminum–colored material.

While all sorts of detonators, igniters, and boosters were employed to explode demolitions, the No.8 detonator was the most common, and was used by the US, UK and many other countries. This is simply the commercial No.8 non-electric blasting cap used the world over. It is a thin-walled copper or aluminum tube 2–2.5in (50–64mm) long and 0.25in (6.5mm) in inside diameter, partly filled with 0.8g of PETN topped with a very small, highly

The British No.7 Mk I press/pull switch, later replaced by the No.13 Mk I. It could be activated by pressure on the round top plate or the rod extension, or by a pull-wire attached to one of the holes in the pressure plate. Compare with Plate B5 showing the earlier No.5 pressure-only switch. (David Gordon Collection)

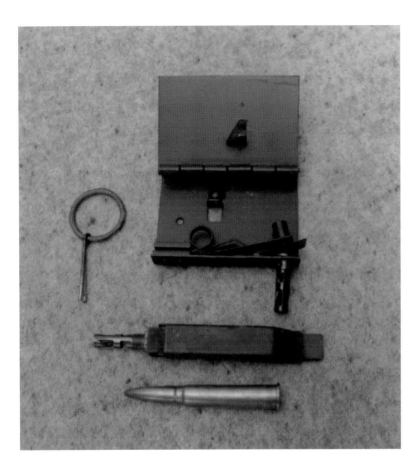

LEFT
Two simple British pressure-release switches.
(Top) The No.3 Mk I is shown open, as if the removal of a weight on the hinged "lid" had allowed the two-part leaf spring to force the tongue out of its path and activate the striker, firing the detonator – see Plate B3.
(Bottom) The No.6 Mk I, with the fuse adapter to the left, and at the right the tapered tongue of the hinged top, for insertion under a weight – see Plate B6. (David Gordon Collection)

BELOW
Two British No.10 Mk I "time pencils," 5in/127mm long; the colored safety tabs indicating the particular time delay can be seen beside the inspection holes, through which the operator checked to see that the striker had not released before he armed the device. Black tabs indicated a delay (at 25°C/77°F) of 10 minutes; red, 19 mins; green, 3 hrs 10 mins; yellow, 6 hrs 30 mins; and blue, 14 hrs 30 minutes. However, for variations see commentary to Plate D1b. A safety fuse or blasting cap could be crimped to the fuse adaptor (top left, bottom right).

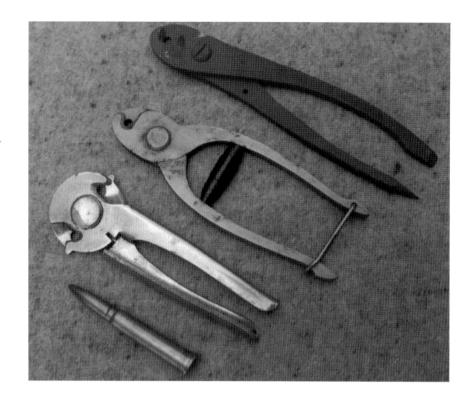

Fuse-crimpers – the upper example is the US M2, the other two are British. These were used to crimp blasting caps/detonators onto safety fuse, detcord, or the fuse adapters on firing devices, as well as to cut safety fuse and detcord. On the handle ends the M2 also has a screwdriver head, and a punch for threading detcord through plastic explosive charges. (David Gordon Collection)

sensitive initiator charge of fulminated mercury, potassium chlorate, and antimony sulphite. One end of the tube is open to allow a length of safety fuse or detcord to be inserted and crimped in place, the closed end being either flat or slightly convex or concave.

Electric blasting caps required either a battery or a blasting machine to detonate via an electrical firing wire. They were little used for assault demolitions owing to the danger of their being set off by static electricity or nearby lightning discharges. They also required a well-trained demolitionist with a full understanding of electrical systems, so were generally unsuitable for use by resistance groups.

Incendiaries

While blowing things to pieces will certainly do the job in most cases, there are times when it is preferable not to be so noisy, and there are targets that can be adequately destroyed or disabled by fire. A simple match can be used to initiate a fire ("lifeboat" or storm matches, resistant to damp and wind, were issued), but some igniter is needed to ensure that the fire catches. This might be of flammable materials, chemical compounds, accelerants such as petroleum products or sulfuric acid and water, or combinations of chlorate, sugar, sodium peroxide, powdered aluminum or magnesium, sulfur, tar, pitch, alcohol, paraffin, etc. Saboteurs and agents were taught how to use the most common of the countless flammable liquids to start destructive fires; how to make gasoline (petrol), aviation and diesel fuels burn hotter and longer; and how to make them adhere to surfaces by thickening them with non-detergent soap, motor oil, and so on.

One of the most effective incendiaries was thermite, a mixture of finely powdered aluminum and iron oxide. An improved form is thermate, with barium nitrate added; when thermate is ignited it burns with an intense white flame at 4,330°F (2,387°C), allowing it to melt through steel (for comparison, an oxyacetylene cutting torch burns at 6,296°F (3,480°C)). Powdered magnesium also burns extremely bright and hot – 4,200°F (2,315°C); when mixed with aluminum powder, charcoal, sulfur, and metallic hydrides it is used for flares, but it too can be used as an incendiary. Since they produce their own oxygen while burning, both thermite and magnesium will even burn underwater.

Some use was made of white phosphorus (WP). This is a soft, waxy, yellow compound that ignites when it comes in contact with air; upon ignition it burns with an intense, 5,000°F (2,760°C) yellow-white flame and produces dense white smoke, which makes it excellent for screening purposes. WP grenades contain a small bursting charge to rupture the casing and scatter the burning compound; this has a putrid odor, and though non-toxic when inhaled, WP particles will poison food and water if they come into direct contact. Besides screening and target-marking, WP was used to ignite fires, though its properties made it diffcult to transport safely.

Firing devices

Firing devices – or in the British term, "switches" – were crucial to the effective employment of both booby traps and sabotage devices; they came in many varieties, and were often employed ingeniously. These small devices might be mechanical, or might function by means of chemical delay or metal deterioration. If mechanical, they were initiated by pull, tension-release, pressure, or pressure-release action.

They usually had a threaded fixture that allowed them to be fitted to standard demolition charges, grenades (replacing the delay fuse), or mines, this threading being standardized between many demolition items. It held a primer or percussion cap that was fired by a spring-loaded firing pin. A detonator/blasting cap was fitted below the primer for instantaneous detonation, or a length of safety fuse of the desired delay time was fitted with a blasting cap on the end. British devices had tube-like adapter sleeves with slots and prongs for fuse to be inserted or a blasting cap to be crimped on. There was at least one arming or safety pin that was removed once the device was ready; many had two pins for more positive safety (there were, of course, instances when careless or hurried individuals failed to remove one of the pins, making the device useless.) To disarm such a device, only one pin had to be re-inserted; in the absence of issue arming pins a small nail or short length of thin, stiff wire could be used.

Pull devices were activated by tugging on a tripwire, which released a spring-loaded firing pin; if detected, they could be neutralized simply by cutting the tripwire. A pressure device was activated by e.g. stepping on it or driving a vehicle over it; this is the type of fuze used in landmines. A pressure-release device required a weight to be placed on it before it was manually armed; when the weight was removed, the device detonated. Tension-release (pull-release) devices were also activated by a tripwire, strung taut; when the wire was broken or intentionally cut it triggered the device – consequently, it would detonate if it was mistaken for a conventional pull device, and the wire was cut to disarm it.

Time-delay switches were more involved. These allowed the demolitionist to pick an approximate time for the charge to detonate, either to allow him to get out of the target area, or to trigger it at an opportune moment. Determining the required delay was the problem – for instance, knowing in advance the precise arrival time of a train on a bridge. That level of detailed

A carton of ten British No.9 Mk I time pencils ("L switches"). The safety pin included a white plastic tag with the delay time marked in red, ranging from minutes to days. (David Gordon Collection).

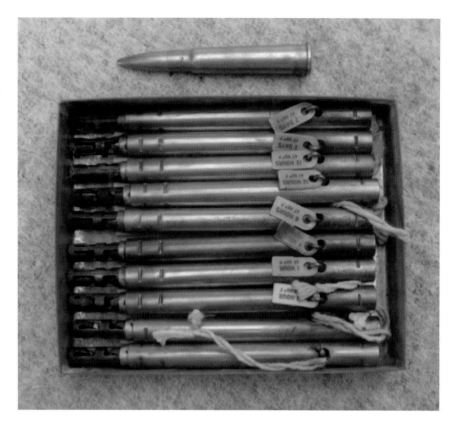

information was seldom known nor could be estimated with enough precision, and neither were such devices sufficiently accurate. However, a time-delay device had the advantage that since it did not have to be triggered by human action – e.g. tripping a tripwire – this allowed the charge to be completely concealed, thus reducing the risk of discovery of an exposed "triggering portion" of the device.

One of the most common was the chemical delay fuze, or "time pencil," initiated by the breaking of an internal glass vial filled with a corrosive liquid, different fuzes being provided for varied delay times. A major complicating factor was that the delay varied greatly depending on the ambient temperature, and it was impossible to calculate for longer delay times when the temperature changed throughout the day and night. The Langley time pencil, or British No.10 switch, was considered the most reliable, and saw the most use by both UK and US personnel. However, as one agent said, "I never knew a single one of these detonators to go off on time," and resistance fighters had to be cautioned not to place too much trust in any of the claimed time delays.

Another type of delay switch depended on the time delay of stretching lead. The fuze held a short, soft lead rod with a groove around it. When the safety pin was removed the lead's own weight stretched it at the groove, and it eventually broke. Yet another type of chemical delay fuze relied on glass ampoules filled with acetone, which when broken by turning a thumbscrew began to dissolve a celluloid disc. The delay time for both these methods depended on temperature, and they had only a plus- or minus-30 and 15 percent accuracy, respectively. For more accurate long delays clockwork timers were preferred.

Sabotage tools

The OSS and SOE developed a number of specialized tools and close-combat weapons for sabotage and espionage purposes. While these may have been somewhat more effective than similar everyday tools, they had their own inherent danger for users. There was, for example, a specially made jacknife with a short "hawk bill" blade ideal for slashing tires, and several types of very effective and compact fighting knives were developed for sentry removal, assassinations, and self-defense; but a kitchen paring knife in a lunch kit or a conventional-looking pocketknife would raise far fewer suspicions if found during a search. There was also a purpose-made garotte; but two short sticks or 3in nails and 18in of thin wire could be assembled quickly, and then disassembled and discarded after use. Some agents and partisans chose not to carry obviously purpose-made devices; to be caught with such things was a sentence of death, after a lengthy and cruel interrogation to find out who had supplied them.

The most commonly used sabotage tools were simply readily available hand implements – hammers, prybars and crowbars, wrenches, pliers, wire- and bolt-cutters, hacksaws, screwdrivers, chisels, punches, knives, hatchets, brush hooks, picks and shovels. Even lengths of pipe, steel rods, poles, planks, bricks or rocks could be used at need to batter equipment.

EXPEDIENT DEVICES AND TECHNIQUES

Agents were taught to concoct their own explosives and incendiaries from commonly available materials. One of the most effective materials for making bulk explosives was ammonia nitrite fertilizer, but unfortunately it was almost impossible to obtain in wartime Europe. Gasoline and oil, two other key ingredients in the saboteur's recipe book, were also difficult to acquire in countries where their distribution was rationed and controlled.

One of the most common and easily-made devices was the "Molotov cocktail" or incendiary bottle. The classic type is simply a glass bottle filled with gasoline, with a length of rag stuffed in the mouth. Before use the bottle is tipped to allow the rag wick to soak up gasoline; the wick is then lit, and the bottle thrown at the target. The bottle breaks upon impact, scattering the gasoline and igniting its vapor.

However, Molotov cocktails do not produce the massive fireballs depicted by Hollywood; the gasoline vapor does not explode unless confined in a partly empty container with the void space filled with vapor, and even then it is only a rather small "explosion." If broken on an engine cover or open vision port, Molotovs may have been effective against the simple AFVs of the 1930s, but they had little effect on more advanced types. Most tank fuel systems were protected from external flames and flash effects, and little if any of the burning gasoline seeped into the tank's interior, which is necessary if it is to be effective. Molotovs produce insufficient smoke to blind a tank crew unless some form of smoke-producing additive like oil is mixed in. They can set light to the tires of wheeled armored vehicles and the rubber track-pads of tanks, but while visually impressive this does not always immobilize AFVs. They were more effective against softer targets such as trucks, automobiles, parked aircraft, machinery, buildings and other light structures – targets more to a saboteur's taste. The

gasoline was frequently enhanced by adding diesel fuel, fuel oil, non-detergent soap flakes, paraffin, tar, rubber strips, or other chemical compositions to make it burn hotter and longer, and/or stick to the target or generate more smoke.

Regardless, the Molotov cocktail was still a weapon of last resort. It could be dangerous to the user if spilt gasoline on the bottle's exterior was ignited by the burning wick. Users were cautioned not to handle Molotov cocktails that missed the target and remained intact, until the wick had burned out; unbroken bottles, weakened by the wick's heat and possibly burning fuel on the outside, could shatter when moved. Filled bottles had to be handled carefully, avoiding knocking them against hard objects or each other, and they had to be checked frequently for leaks and evaporation. Nevertheless, desperate for any form of antitank weapon during the invasion fears following Dunkirk in summer 1940, the British Army and Home Guard were trained to make Molotov cocktails (on the instructions of British veterans of the Spanish Civil War International Brigades); one recommended mixture was 25 percent gasoline and 75 percent oil. They also remained in use by the Red Army until quite late in the war.

Punji stakes

Depending on how they are used, *punji* stakes may be classified as either booby traps or tactical obstacles. The following are extracts from an article, originally from a British source, that was published in the US Army's *Intelligence Bulletin* in October 1944:

"Punjis – bamboo or other wood spikes sharpened to a needle point – are formidable weapons. They ... have been adopted by certain

This is a rather superior version of the "Molotov cocktail," as still issued by the Red Army quite late in the war. It has two glass tubes of sulfuric acid taped to the sides; when the bottle was thrown the tubes would also break, and the acid reacted with and ignited the gasoline. This widely-used expedient device, particularly associated with the Russo-Finnish Winter War (1939–40), was originally named as a jeer against the Soviet Foreign Minister Vyacheslav Molotov, whom the Finns held to be in large measure responsible for the war. The Red Army called it simply a *butylkas goryuchej smes'yu*, "bottle with flammable mixture." The effect on the target was often disappointing; one or even several quart bottles simply do not deliver sufficient gasoline to do much damage to an armored vehicle, even if broken on the engine cover. In the author's personal Army experience of making and testing Molotovs, they were rather unimpressive, although additives helped (once again, readers are strongly urged not to attempt such experiments, which can be extremely dangerous to users, bystanders and property.) (IWM MUN 39)

[Allied] forces for use as jungle traps against the Japanese. It is also reliably reported that the Japanese themselves are employing punjis.

"Ordinary punjis will penetrate thick uniforms or the upper part of a shoe. When the point ... has been hardened in fire, it is even more effective, and can easily penetrate the sole of any shoe issued by the Japanese. Although punji wounds are not necessarily fatal, they are ... extremely painful and do not heal readily. (It is possible that the healing process is delayed by a natural acid in the bamboo.) [One of the aims of punjis is to cause casualties that must be treated and evacuated.] Blood poisoning has been known to result from punji wounds, particularly in cases where jungle tribesmen have placed spoiled meat on the needle point of the punji [human or animal faeces were also smeared on the stakes].

"Punji traps are most effectively placed when they are merged with natural jungle obstacles. In the defense, they may be used either as barricades around camps or as barriers to impede the advance of an attacking force. In the offense, they may be constructed behind enemy lines to stop or hinder any retreat. Enemy patrols can be disbanded by a skillful use of these traps in conjunction with covering snipers. Here are a few of the ways in which punjis are used.

"Punji pits – A pit, 4–6 feet deep, 4–6 feet long, and 3–4 feet wide, is dug in the middle of a jungle trail or at a stream crossing. Smaller holes may be dug, large enough for a foot to enter. A number of long, sharp punjis are placed upright in this pit, with their fire-hardened points slightly below ground level. The pit is concealed by a flimsy lid, which is nothing more than a bamboo lattice covered with a few creepers. Last of all, a natural camouflage garnish of mud or leaves is applied... Anyone falling into the pit is instantly impaled on the spikes.

"Similarly, a slit trench can be so placed that attacking Japanese will be likely to utilize it. Like the cover of the punji pit, the bottom of this trench is false, and underneath it there are sharp punjis, which will pierce the shoes of the Japanese when they jump into the trench.

"Bamboo whip – A 3-inch bamboo pole can be bent back across a jungle path in such a way that when it is released, the force of the blow will kill a man walking along the path. To ensure effective result, punji spikes can be attached at the end of the whip. The whip is held in position by a bamboo creeper or by wire, with a peg at the end of the wire pressing against two horizontal sticks. Contact with a tripwire across the path withdraws the longer stick, allowing the heavy bamboo to whip forcefully across the path. If the tripwire is covered with leaves, and if the bamboo whip is concealed by branches, the Japanese are much less likely to detect the trap.

"Punjis for camp defense – For the purposes of local defense, a camp in the jungle is sometimes built in the form of a triangle, with a large tree at each apex. The perimeter of the camp is surrounded by a punji wall, 6 feet in depth and varying from 4 inches to 6 feet in height... Gates are protected with bamboo sharpened at each end, bent in a U-shape, and so placed that the sharp ends point outward. Slit trenches, to be occupied in case of attack, are dug along the inner side of the fence. Lookouts posted in the trees at the apexes of the triangle act as snipers in case of attack.

"Other punji traps – Punjis placed under water in a river or at a beach, with the points 2 inches below the surface, will rule out swimming as an enemy mode of travel and will puncture the bottoms of ordinary native river boats.

"Sometimes a bamboo knife, pointing downward, is attached to the far side (from the expected enemy approach) of a low limb overhanging a jungle trail. A man bending low to pass beneath the limb will receive a severe wound in the back when he straightens up.

"Punjis may also be prepared by snipers lying in wait to ambush hostile patrols. Along the sides of the trail or other canalized approach that a hostile patrol is likely to use, sharpened bamboo spikes, 18 inches long, are placed at intervals of about 1 foot and are pointed toward the trail at an angle of 45 degrees. When the hostile patrol appears, it is fired on by hidden snipers. On hearing the first shots, the instinctive reaction of the members of the patrol is to seek cover. If they dart into the growth beside the trail, they are impaled on the bamboo spikes."

EMPLOYMENT

Concealment

Many factors had to be taken into consideration for the employment of booby traps and sabotage devices.

Naturally, sabotage materials had to be hidden in order to be effective. Ideally they would look like something innocent, but achieving this was difficult, so simple concealment was relied upon. Often they were painted olive drab, dark green, khaki, or black. Painting them in other colors might have helped some look more like a civilian item, at a cursory glance, but this was seldom done. They and their cartons and inner packaging seldom bore markings of any kind, neither designations nor serial or stock numbers.

ALLIED HAND GRENADES

Hand grenades were widely used by resistance and partisan groups for booby-trapping and sabotage as well as for their usual purpose, and some types were also employed as demolition charges. When used for booby-trapping they still had their usual 4- or 5-second delay fuse, which hampered their effectiveness to some degree: if the soldier tripping the grenade was aware of it, he might have time to seek cover or at least hit the ground, surviving unscathed or with only minor wounds.

1: US Mk II "pineapple" fragmentation grenade. The most common means of employment as a booby trap was simply to fasten the grenade to a tree, barbed-wire picket, stake, or other suitable fixed object with wire or tape; anchor a tripwire to another fixed object; and attach the tripwire to the ring of the cotter pin – ensuring the pin was straightened and even partially pulled out. Very occasionally, nails or scrap metal were taped or wired to the grenade to increase the fragmentation.

2: British No.36M "Mills bomb." Another method was to dig a small hole in which the grenade was laid on its side with the arming lever upwards. The hole extended to one side to allow access so that the arming pin could be removed, and space had to be allowed at the grenade's fuze end to permit the arming lever to rotate fully. A sufficiently weighty and enticing object was placed on top to hold the lever in place, the pin was removed with extreme caution, and the trap was camouflaged.

3a: British No.75 "Hawkins grenade." The No.75 and No.82 (below) were two British special-purpose antitank grenades supplied to resistance groups by the SOE, and also used by US paratroopers and Rangers. The No.75, mass-produced from June 1942, could be used as a grenade, mine, booby trap, or demolition charge.

3b: "French charge." Here two Hawkins grenades connected by detcord are buried in the ballast beneath a railroad track, to be activated – again via detcord – when a train passes over standard railroad fog-signal detonators (**3c** – here two of them, to ensure detonation.) Two or more No.75s would shatter a lengthy rail section, to increase the chance of derailing the locomotive.

4a: British No.82 "Gammon bomb." Introduced in May 1943; up to 1.9lb/0.9kg of any available pliable explosive could be molded into a ball and inserted into the bag through the elasticated bottom hem – such as two 8oz No.2 PE cartridges (**4b**). A No.8 blasting cap/detonator set in a booster pellet (see cutaway, **4c**) was initiated by a No.247 "All Ways" fuze (**4d**); when the safety cap was removed and the grenade was thrown, the weighted tape unwound to pull out the loose arming pin, and thereafter the charge exploded on impact. This made it deadly in ambushes, but with a full antitank charge its throwing-range was short, and lighter charges had to be used if it was to reach any distance. On some occasions, for antipersonnel use, nails, gravel or scrap metal would be pressed into a half-charge of PE before inserting it in the bag.

1

2

3a

3c

3b

4d

4a

4b

P.E. No. 2

4c

Nº 82-1

Concealing explosives for clandestine transport: this is a display in the Explosives Camouflage Section at the exhibition room maintained behind locked doors at the Natural History Museum in West Kensington, London. It seems to show both explosive blocks and cartons of time pencils, and hollow fake bricks and cinder blocks. The European resistance movements had to be supplied with tens of thousands of tons of explosive each month, so it was an advantage if they could be moved around concealed in bulk-cargo items such as these. (IWM HU61180)

Sabotage items were concealed by many means when transporting them to the objective site. They could be hidden in clothing or taped to the body beneath clothing; hidden in luggage, or in hidden compartments in other forms of container or package; concealed among bulk cargo (raw foods, construction materials, and other bulk goods); hidden inside items (automobile spare tires, hollowed-out books), and so on. Some explosive items were disguised to look like something else entirely; they were camouflaged as anything from cigarettes to sugar beets, Chinese stone lanterns or wood carvings, and horse, cow, camel, and donkey droppings. There was even an explosive called "Aunt Jemima" – the brand name for a pancake mix – made of 25 percent flour and 75 percent RDX to look like flour (it was even claimed to be bakeable and edible, but the ingredients of RDX are poisonous.) In theory, plastic explosives could be molded, with the addition of Vaseline, into innocuous-seeming objects, thus allowing them to be smuggled through German checkpoints, but it is not known if this was actually attempted. Various types of vegetables were replicated from hollow plaster or papier-mâché and realistically painted, allowing small-arms ammunition, detonators, firing devices, and explosives to be smuggled. Methods for smuggling sabotage materials were limited only by the limits of ingenuity, and German security and counterintelligence personnel had to be just as imaginative to detect them.

As far as was possible, a sabotage device needed to be infiltrated to the target completely assembled and prepared for use in advance, so it could be emplaced rapidly to avoid detection. If it was to be detonated by a time-delay system of any kind, the device could be completely concealed out of sight

(though a burning time fuse might alert the enemy by smell, smoke, or even the faint hissing sound.) If it had to be activated by tripping a firing device then the triggering system did have to be exposed, so it was essential to conceal or disguise this. It is one thing to hide a tripwire in vegetation; it is quite another to disguise it in a factory or aircraft hangar – imagination and resourcefulness were critical.

No matter where or how any sabotage device was emplaced, the site could not appear to be disturbed in any unnatural way. It was obviously important that arming pins, safety clips, packing materials, or other related components not be left lying about. Everything had to appear natural and orderly; even disturbed dust, scuff marks, or a small item out of place could tip off an alert guard or worker.

One technique was to emplace one or more decoy devices, in the hope that after finding these the enemy would cease searching, and fail to find the very well-concealed main change. To be effective the decoys had to use actual explosives and firing devices, and be realistically concealed and placed; if they were found too easily, the search would continue.

Another display at the London exhibition room – SOE Station XVb – includes hollow fake turnips, sugar-beets and potatoes, as used for clandestine transport of munitions. Note also the Sten gun magazines at top right. The SOE's camouflage section worked at Station XV, at Borehamwood near London. (IWM HU61185)

Emplacement

Besides concealment, the placing of devices had to ensure that maximum damage was inflicted. Sometimes the needs of concealment and effective placement of charges were contradictory, so a compromise had to be made, but in such cases concealment took priority if there was any chance the area might be inspected. No matter how potentially favorable the placement of a charge, this would be pointless if it were discovered.

Saboteurs needed to be familiar enough with the characteristics and vulnerabilities of particular types of targets to inflict the greatest damage. Agents were taught to damage the same components of multiple vehicles or equipment, so that undamaged parts could not simply be "cannibalized" to repair other vehicles – for example, they were taught always to damage the right drive-wheel piston cylinder of locomotives, not the right cylinder on some and the left on others. They were also taught that damaging the simplest parts was often the most effective means of disabling targets, since these were usually the easiest and quickest to damage.

Sabotaging vehicles and machinery

On vehicles, for example, the simplest methods included cutting fan belts, coolant hoses, oil and brake lines and brake cables. Radiators could be punctured, as well as fuel tanks. To prevent the splashing of leaking fuel from attracting attention, sand, earth, sawdust, rags, or sacking could be piled beneath the punctured tank. While destroying or severely damaging any enemy vehicle was beneficial, given the Germans' shortages in transport, it was particularly valuable to target special-purpose vehicles. These included ammunition trucks, radio trucks, command vehicles, fuel trucks, water trucks and trailers in the desert and other arid areas, and field kitchen trailers in wintertime. (During the Winter War, 1939–40, the Finns degraded a Soviet division to the point where it became combat-ineffective by specifically targeting its 50-plus kitchen trailers with hit-and-run raids, thus denying the troops hot food and drink in extremely cold conditions.)

One purpose-made item was the tire spike or "crow's-foot"; this was simply a modern version of the ancient caltrop, used since time immemorial to hamper advancing cavalry and infantry. In its World War II form it consisted of two 4in-long steel tubes, or triangular sheet-steel points, bent at 45-degree angles and welded together in such a manner that when dropped on the ground one of the four sharpened ends was always point-upward to

B BRITISH BOOBY-TRAP SWITCHES
British firing devices, commonly referred to as "switches," were operated by pull, pressure, or pressure-release. They were designed for use with demolition charges and some mines, but – unlike their US counterparts – they could not be fitted into hand grenades. They incorporated a striker and percussion cap, but a No.8 detonator could also be inserted into the fuse adapter; detcord or time-delay safety fuse was crimped in as needed. These devices were widely used by the OSS, as similar American devices were not introduced until late in the war.

1: No.1 switch. This tubular pull device, with the tripwire ring on the upper end, measured 4in × ⅝in.

2: No.2 switch. A tubular pressure-detonated device mounted on a small base plate, measuring 4⅝in × 1½in. It required a pressure of 30–40lb to detonate.

3: No.3 switch. This pressure-release type consisted of a small rectangular box, 3in × 2in, with a tongue angled down from the hinged "lid" to hold back a spring-loaded striker. An object weighing at least 1½lb had to be placed on the lid before the safety pin could be removed. Lifting the weight allowed the

spring to force the tongue back and up, so the striker pin struck the percussion cap or detonator in the end of the fuse-adapter tube.

4: No.4 switch. Another pull-type switch similar to the No.1, but very slightly smaller and much simplified; it had two anchoring eyes, and required a pull of 6–8lb.

5: No. 5 switch. This pressure-activated device, measuring 3¾in × 1¼in, was of more complex design than the No.2. It consisted of a rectangular housing with a pressure plate on top, hinged at the end holding the fuse adapter. A 2½in extension rod with a 1¼in bushing could be screwed into the pressure plate to facilitate it being placed under railroad track, floorboards, etc., its length being adjustable by twisting it (see red arrow). Once it was installed, and armed by removing the pin, its detcord link to the explosive charge was concealed with gravel, etc. To set it off required 21lb of pressure near the free end, or 50–60lb at the hinge end.

6: No.6 switch. This pressure-release type, measuring 4½in × ⅝in, had a hinged release lever on top of the housing. The free end of the lever had a small tongue, allowing it to be slipped beneath almost any object weighing at least 6lb.

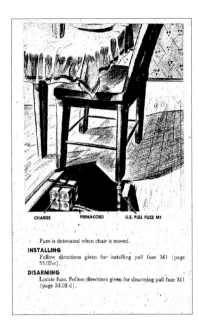

CHARGE   PRIMACORD   U.S. PULL FUZE M1

Fuze is detonated when chair is moved.

INSTALLING
Follow directions given for installing pull fuze M1 (page 53.02-c).

DISARMING
Locate fuze. Follow directions given for disarming pull fuze M1 (page 53.02-d).

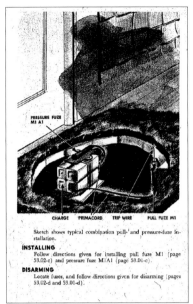

PRESSURE FUZE M1 A1

CHARGE   PRIMACORD   TRIP WIRE   PULL FUZE M1

Sketch shows typical combination pull-and pressure-fuze installation.

INSTALLING
Follow directions given for installing pull fuze M1 (page 53.02-c) and pressure fuze M1A1 (page 53.01-c).

DISARMING
Locate fuzes, and follow directions given for disarming (pages 53.02-d and 53.01-d).

TRIP WIRE ATTACHED TO CEMENT BAG   PULL FUZE M1   PRIMACORD   CHARGE

Sack of cement or other material is booby trapped as shown in sketch.

INSTALLING
Follow directions given for installing U. S. pull fuze M1 (page 53.02-c).

DISARMING
Locate fuze and follow directions given for disarming (page 53.02-d).

Cutaway illustrations of fairly elaborate booby-traps, which would have taken Allied troops more time to install than most tactical situations would allow or justify. In each case four 1lb TNT blocks are used – such large charges, far greater than needed to kill the individual triggering the trap, were recommended so as to cause as many casualties and as widespread damage as possible.
(Left) The charge under the floorboards is linked to an M1 pull-firing device and, via a hole drilled through the floor, to a chairleg; it will detonate if the chair is moved.
(Centre) The charge is under the floor of an outside porch; an M1A1 pressure-firing device is fitted directly above the charge, and an M1 pull-firing device is wired to the doormat through a drilled hole, so that the charge will also detonate if the mat is moved.
(Right) Wire from an M1 pull-firing device passes up through the floor and is attached to cement bags stacked above the charge. Any stacked materials of use to the enemy could be used as bait – rations, ammunition boxes, etc.

pierce tires. In the absence of purpose-made crow's-feet, nails placed at an angle under the tires of parked vehicles were quick and easy to place – a nail could be inserted into a small matchbox and this could be wedged upright under the front of a rear tire. Tires were best slashed on the side, making a cut several inches long; side-slashed tires could not be repaired, and all rubber was a scarce strategic material. Simple punctures were not as effective, and simply removing the valve stem was only an inconvenience. (One wartime expedient tire repair commonly practiced by the Russians was to pack grass tightly into the tire.)

Given more time and access, a vehicle could be disabled by removing a sparkplug, inserting a small metal bolt or nut, and replacing the plug. When introduced into the fuel, lubricating oil, or coolant supply of vehicle engines or other machinery, abrasives such as sand, emery dust, pumice or metal filings, and softer clogging materials like sawdust, shredded waste cotton, wool, or even paper, could do irreparable damage. Even cereal or rice grains introduced into fuel swelled, and choked the fuel line. Just three or four spoonfuls or lumps of sugar or a small bottle of linseed oil in the fuel tank would ruin an engine after it had traveled a few kilometers; this not only caused it to seize up, but irreparably damaged many components, thus preventing repair by the simple replacement of individual parts. One pint of water, wine, urine, paint, cleaning fluids or other liquids added to 20 gallons/80 liters of gasoline will dilute the fuel to the point where combustion cannot be achieved, making it necessary to flush and clean the entire fuel system. Wax, paraffin, sawdust, clay, rubber strips cut from inner tubes, rubber bands and cut-up pencil erasers, even finely shredded paper ruins the fuel and the engine as well. Introducing low-flashpoint oil to diesel fuel will have the same effect. When placing abrasives and other solids into a vehicle's oil or fuel system, agents were taught to first remove the filler-cap filter if possible, or to use a screwdriver to punch a hole through it. Ball bearings were in short supply, and factories producing them were a priority target of the Allied bombing campaign; bearings could also be destroyed quickly by introducing abrasives into their lubricating oil.

Explosive and incendiary charges used against vehicles and aircraft would be placed to destroy the engines, transmissions, and instrument panels, and to set fire to fuel, ammunition, and tires. Damaging the elevators on an aircraft's horizontal tail stabilizer with small charges (or even manually) required little effort, but prevented it from taking off. Large weapons such as artillery pieces were vulnerable to comparatively small charges placed to destroy the recoil and recuperator (recoil return) cylinders, sights, and breech blocks. Again, when destroying a number of weapons the same components had to be damaged on all, so that parts could not be salvaged to repair others. This also applied when sabotaging power plants, generators, communications equipment and heavy machinery.

Railroads, bridges and power lines

Railroads were key targets, and relatively easy to attack, since it was impossible to guard the thousands of kilometers of cross-country track even if stations and rail yards were well secured.

At the simplest, coating both rails on a track with axle grease or tar could halt a train, especially on a gradient; a long stretch had to be greased, as locomotives were equipped to release sand on icy or wet rails for traction, but they only carried moderate amounts. In Western Europe rails were mostly bolted to metal or concrete crossties (sleepers) rather than spiked to wooden crossties as in the US and USSR; rails could therefore be unbolted and left in place on the loosened sleepers and fishplates – preferably on a curve – to derail a train.

Rails were relatively brittle and required only a small charge to break them. A cut rail could be repaired quickly, in 2–4 hours, but this was enough to make a shambles of train schedules, especially on lines with few alternative tracks for rerouting. Many cuts throughout a rail system over a given timeframe could severely back up the traffic, preventing timely delivery of troops and supplies. Destruction of switches (points), crossings, signal boxes, telegraph lines, coaling and watering points, and related facilities would further hamper traffic. The delay and difficulty of repairing cut tracks could be extended by the wise placement of charges. Instead of placing one at just any point on a track, placing it at a joint damaged two lengths of rail, and doing this on a curve meant that replacement rails of the necessary

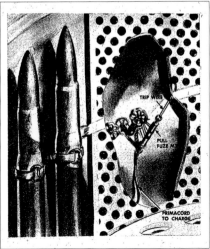

LEFT
An M1A1 pressure fuze and four 1lb TNT blocks are hidden inside a truck's seat cushion. Anyone unfortunate enough to sit on it would be blown to shreds, as would the truck. This size of charge would be very wasteful for resistance saboteurs seeking to destroy a single vehicle, unless it was a high-priority target like a crane or repair-shop truck – normally, a handful of sugar in the fuel tank would be much more cost-effective.

RIGHT
Cutaway instructional drawing for booby-trapping an abandoned tank: charges are hidden behind stowed 75mm shells in the turret basket, and linked by detcord to a pull-release device anchored to valves on the hull wall. If the turret is rotated, the trap will detonate.

curve-radius had to be brought in. The rail on the outside of the curve was the preferred one to break, as a moving train's momentum carried it outwards on a curve, further ensuring derailment. Training diagrams often show multiple charges attached to a rail and linked by detcord, but it did little good to cut a single rail into four pieces with three charges – it could still be replaced by a single rail. It was better to place detcord-linked charges on four different sections, so they all had to be replaced.

Tunnels were tempting but impractical targets, since their effective destruction required massive amounts of explosive. Bridges were primary targets; if destroyed or severely damaged they could cause the enemy a great deal of trouble, but even relatively small bridges were difficult targets owing to their heavy construction. It required a lot of explosive to destroy even a small culvert-type bridge, and it was time-consuming to emplace. Bridges were also fairly easy for the enemy to guard, and their exposed structure made it almost impossible to conceal charges and firing wires from attentive patrols.

Saboteurs often had limited amounts of explosive, or could only carry so much to the target. The effectiveness of charges could be increased by tamping – packing sandbags atop the charges to direct their blast toward the structure to be destroyed. To minimize the quantity of explosives used to destroy bridges, formulas were available for calculating the necessary amount. However, to arrive at a precise solution the user needed accurate dimensions for the beams, pilings, and stringers; typically, saboteurs simply estimated these dimensions, read off the recommended amount – and added to it, just to be certain.

Telephone, telegraph, and power lines and their poles were easy to cut, and – since they were placed alongside roads and rail tracks – easily accessible. Only wire- or bolt-cutters were necessary (although they needed to be insulated if cutting power lines), plus a ladder or pole-climbers. Ideally a lengthy section would be cut and dragged off to prevent repairmen from simply splicing the cut line back together. Damaging line equipment such as transformers and junction boxes was even more effective, since they were more time-consuming to replace. (A consideration before cutting such lines was that it might create more of an inconvenience for civilians, upon whom the resistance relied for support, than it did for the enemy.)

C US FIRING DEVICES

American booby-trap firing devices did not see service until 1943. Regardless of design, all possessed a common threaded fuse fitting that matched the fuse wells of hand grenades, TNT charges and landmines, allowing them to be turned into booby traps. The devices could be used in training without a blasting cap being fitted to the fuse adapters; when triggered, only the small igniting primer would pop, to let an errant soldier know that he had better improve his skills.

1a and 1b: M1 pull firing device. Requiring a pull of 3–5lb, this was one of the most widely used, in two versions; the later (**1b**) differed in having a differently manufactured housing and an anchoring eye, and possessed a "positive safety" – the lower cotter pin. An example of its use is depicted as (**1c**), replacing the firing mechanism of a grenade taped to a post, 2–3ft above ground.

2: M1 combination firing device. This had a pressure-plate plunger (20–40lb pressure) at the end, in addition to a side-pull firing release for a tripwire (3–6lb pull). It could be used with the M2 and M3 antipersonnel mines, as well as with grenades and demolition charges rigged as booby traps.

3: M1 pressure-release firing device. This had the same cross-section dimensions as the ½lb and 1lb TNT block charges, allowing them to be fitted to its side. These were widely used as mine antitampering charges, as shown here set beneath an M1A1 antitank mine.

4a and 4b: M1 pressure firing device. A horizontal tubular housing with the plunger on the side. Early models (**4a**) had a rectangular base plate, and later ones (**4b**) anchor flanges and a "positive safety" pin.

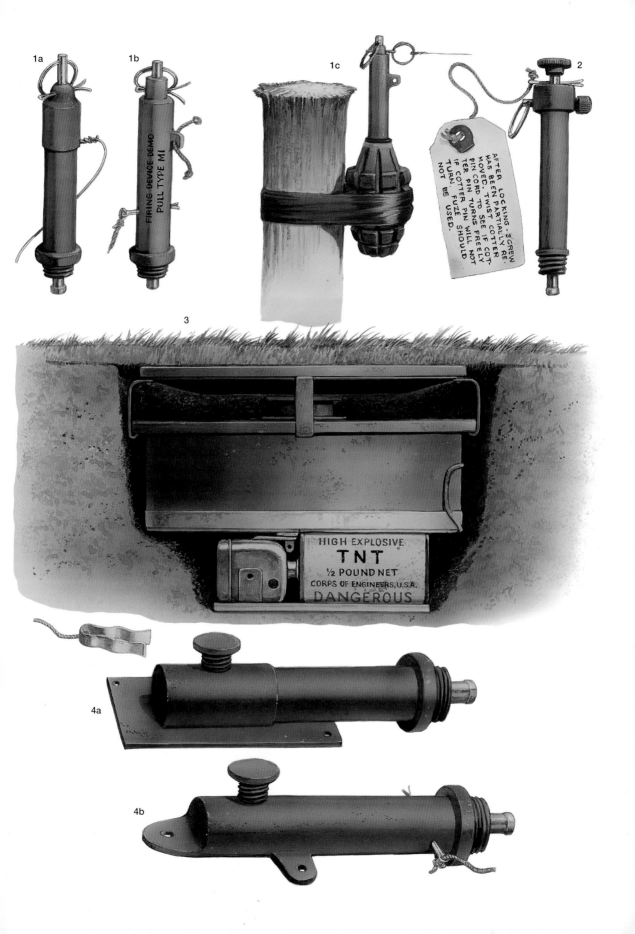

1a

1b

FIRING DEVICE DEMO. PULL TYPE MI

1c

2

AFTER LOCKING-SCREW HAS BEEN PARTIALLY RE-MOVED, TWIST COTTER PIN CORD TO SEE IF COT-TER PIN TURNS FREELY. IF COTTER PIN WILL NOT TURN, FUZE SHOULD NOT BE USED.

3

HIGH EXPLOSIVE
TNT
½ POUND NET
CORPS OF ENGINEERS, U.S.A.
DANGEROUS

4a

4b

On the SOE's industrial sabotage course at Station XVII, trainee agents are shown how to disable an electricity transformer. Sabotaging such central facilities achieved far more than repeated cutting of power lines. For instance, targeted French Resistance sabotage of its power supply stations brought production at the Schneider-Creusot arms factory near Lyons to a halt – something that RAF Bomber Command had not been able to achieve, despite killing some 1,000 French civilians in its attempts. (IWM MH24430)

Installing tripwires

While string or thin cord could be used as tripwire, issue tripwires were usually made of semi-flexible steel, sometimes painted green or sand-color. Wire was usually issued on wooden spools, together with firing devices and mines.

The tripwire was uncoiled from its spool and attached first to the anchor farthest from the booby trap; this attachment to a post, tree, or other fixed object had to be firm to ensure that it would not pull free. Ankle- to knee-high was the common height, but in some areas wires had to be placed high enough off the ground to prevent small animals from tripping them (on some Pacific islands, for example, rats and land crabs were a problem.) The wire was then run towards the booby trap, ensuring that it was concealed as well as possible; the result had to be examined from a short distance and from the direction the enemy would approach, and the camouflage was rearranged and the wire rerouted if necessary. It was then carefully attached to the unarmed firing device, leaving a little slack in the wire – a wire too tautly strung might activate the firing device when the safety pin was removed.

Some devices had two safety pins; the arming pin was removed first, and if there was a "positive safety" pin, this was removed last. If the device activated when the arming pin was removed, the positive safety pin still blocked the released striker; if this occurred the tripwire was unfastened, and the device was unscrewed from the charge and replaced. Tension-release wires were necessarily taut so as to be activated when cut. The area was then examined again, and any packaging or other signs of disturbance were removed. Leaving the whole scene in its natural state was particularly important if an unsuspecting enemy was intended to move an object in a normal manner, such as opening a door. If it was to be a "baited" booby trap, some desirable item was arranged to tempt an enemy to pick it up. All personnel were cleared from the area, with the arming pin being removed at the last moment and carried away.

Booby-trapping mines

Landmines were frequently booby-trapped to make their removal hazardous, inflict casualties on mine removal personnel, and slow the clearance process; in fact, mine booby-trapping was the most common use of such traps by the Allies. These antilifting or antitampering devices were generally simple. They had to be installed rapidly and safely, preferably using only limited materials; it was realized that more often than not they would be discovered, and there was no sense in wasting resources and time on elaborate and intricate traps.

The first deceptive aspect of mine booby-trapping was irregularity. It was usually prescribed that mines be laid in precise patterns specific distances apart, to aid their recovery and clearing by friendly personnel. However, once the enemy had discovered a few of the mines they could discern the pattern, simplifying their task. It was not necessary to booby-trap every mine; once the enemy found that booby-trapped mines were present, every mine had to be treated as such. Obviously, mines were selected for booby-trapping to no discernible ratio or pattern in a minefield, and different means of booby-trapping would be employed in the same minefield to further

A pair of Soviet partisans emplace a demolition charge contained in a wooden box under a timber bridge. The right-hand man holds a length of safety fuse with a blasting cap attached. (Nik Cornish Collection)

confuse clearing parties. Mostly antitank mines were booby-trapped, but occasionally so were antipersonnel mines. Only small demolition charges of a ½lb or less were generally used, as were hand grenades; the small charge had only to initiate the mine's explosive charge via sympathetic detonation. However, sometimes mortar or artillery shells were used, either recovered duds or rounds defective for firing; this conserved resources, and created a bigger bang.

Mines were normally buried and well camouflaged, but hasty minefields were sometimes laid in which mines were unburied. They were either simply laid on the ground, or partly buried to at least half their depth, or to their full depth with their tops flush with the ground – this prevented them from being washed away by heavy rains. Such mines were seldom booby-trapped; they were intended to limit or channel enemy movement, and would be recovered when the laying unit moved on. It was sometimes noted that German troops indicated booby-trapped mines by a certain positioning of the carrying-handle on the mine's side, for the later guidance of their own engineers. It is

---

D

TIME-DELAY DEVICES

A variety of these were available, but most of them were relatively inaccurate, since they were affected by changing temperatures. The longer the delay time, and the wider the change in temperature during the interval between activation and initiation, the greater the degree of inaccuracy; it was advised that two time-delay fuses be attached to a charge to ensure detonation.

1a: M1 delay firing device. One of the devices most commonly used by both the UK and US was the British-designed Langley "time pencil," 5in long × ¼in diameter. This US version had the standard crimp-on adapter, and was issued in a carton of ten. It was activated by crushing the thin copper tube at the top end, which contained a glass vial of corrosive. There was an inspection hole above the adapter into which the user looked to ensure the striker had not been released. Once the device was activated the colored safety strip was removed; this also identified the (theoretical) delay time.

1b: British No.10 "time pencil." This had a slotted tubular adapter that allowed safety fuse to be inserted, or a blasting cap crimped on with safety fuse or detcord inserted. They were issued in a metal can containing five "pencils," with tabs all color-coded for the same delay. To give an idea of the gross variances in delay time: the yellow-coded device detonated after 2 hours at 109.5°F; at 77°F it took 6 hrs 30 mins; at 32°F, 28 hrs; and at -4°F, it did not go off for 10 days.

2: British No.9 delay switch. This operated on the principle that tellurium lead stretches at a uniform rate (though this too varies depending on the temperature); when a lead component broke it released a spring-loaded striker. The safety pin had a tag identifying ten different delays in hours or days. They were accurate plus or minus 30 percent if the delay was under 24 hours, and longer delay switches were more accurate. Disadvantages were that they had to be installed vertically to operate properly, and the pin could not be reinserted once they were activated. The tube measured 4⅜in × ⅜in diameter.

3a: British AC Mk I acetone-celluloid delay device. This came in a tin box (**3d**), complete with a booster charge (**3b**) and six acetone-filled glass ampoules (**3c**), each with a different delay time (at 20°C/69°F) indicated by the color – red (4 hours), orange (7 hrs), yellow (14 hrs), green (22 hrs 30 mins), blue (36 hrs), and violet (4½ days). The thumbscrew-end was removed, the ampoule inserted, and when the safety pin was removed the thumbscrew was turned to crush the ampoule; the acetone ate through a celluloid disc at an approximately predictable rate, to release a spring-loaded firing pin. It was mainly intended for underwater use with limpet mines, and had a different type of threaded adapter than other firing devices.

4: Mk III clockwork delay device. One of the most common of a number of different clockwork firing devices was this small British-designed Mk III, also made in the US; both US and UK fuse adapters could be fitted. Waterproof to 20ft and usable with limpet mines, it could be set for delays of between 15 mins and 11 hrs 45 minutes. The housing measured 2¾in × 2½in × 1½in; the controls were on the back, normally covered by masking tape.

5a and 5b: Improvised delay devices. A much simpler initiation system could be made from a burning cigarette and a book of matches with the cover torn off (in **5a**, a French propaganda piece, with sabotage instructions for using a rail spike to derail a train). Here it is tied below a sprinkler head on a water pipe; after some minutes the flaring matchbook will activate the sprinkler system, causing confusion and damaging materials and documents. Another method was to tear off the end of a British-type box of matches (**5b**), pull the head end of the matches partly out of the box, and insert a cigarette, before placing the matchbox among flammable materials and lighting the cigarette. (This is a British wartime matchbox by Moreland & Co., with the security slogan "BE LIKE DAD – KEEP MUM"; obviously, it would never be carried by any agent behind enemy lines.) The end of a safety fuse could be inserted in either of these expedient devices for a short-delay ignition.

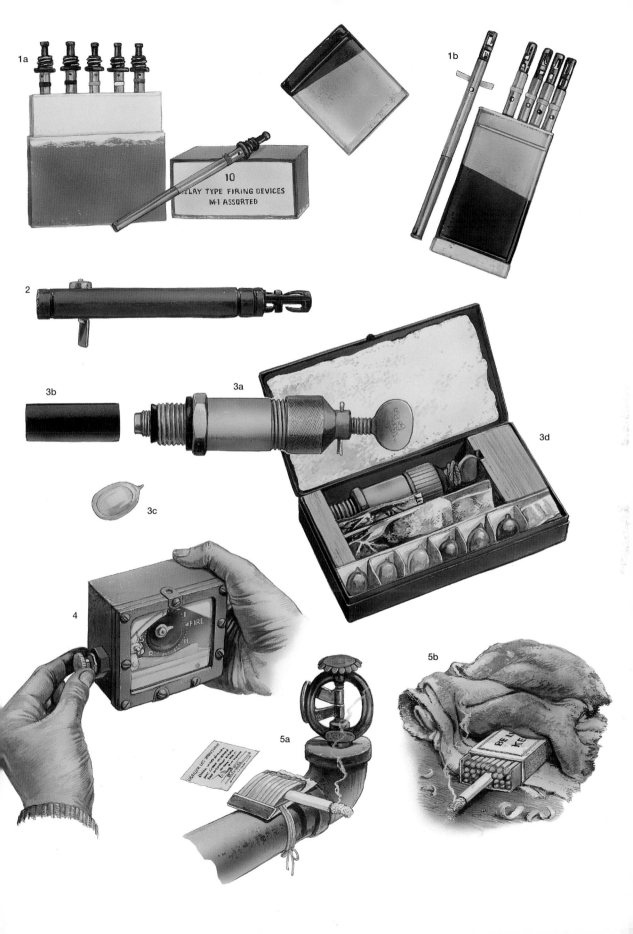

A bridge over the Guil River at Embrun, France, destroyed by the French Resistance. Rather than attempting to blow the heavy vertical pilings, charges could be placed across the center of bridge spans from side to side. A charge sufficient to fracture the deck and the horizontal stringers supporting it would allow the deck to break and collapse under its own weight; even if the bridge failed to collapse fully, its weakened state could prevent its use. The abutments – the brick or masonry retaining walls supporting its ends – were the most massively constructed parts of a bridge; it required huge amounts of explosive to collapse them, but if this could be achieved it made reconstruction even more difficult and time-consuming. (IWM HU57103)

not known if the Allies did anything like this, but it is possible; the practice would have been developed by a particular unit and would not have been found in manuals.

The booby trap was usually placed beneath or to the side of the mine. In rare instances one or more other mines were linked to a booby-trapped mine by detcord for simultaneous detonation. The booby-trap charge might be activated by a pull-firing device attached to the mine, or by a pressure-release device activated when the mine was lifted off it. A more sophisticated method was to position a charge with a pressure-release device on its side, with the activating lever against the mine's side surface; failing to discover a booby trap beneath the mine, an engineer might lift it without making an all-round check, with fatal consequences. Some mines had secondary fuse wells for firing devices on the bottom or side; a blasting cap and pull-firing device could be fitted to the secondary fuse well, with a short pull-wire running to a buried anchoring stake beneath or to the side of the mine.

The unit laying the minefield was supposed to make a scaled diagram of the field's layout, with one or more landmarks indicated by direction and distance so the orientation of the field could be determined. Any booby-trapped mines were to be indicated, as was the type of booby trap. Any intentional gaps and lanes for the passage of patrols were also marked. In the "fog of war," however, the shifting and relief of units and the passage of time often led to these diagrams being lost, or a unit failing to pass them to a relieving unit, thus rendering the removal or breaching of "friendly" minefields just as dangerous for them as it was for the enemy.

In order to launch attacks, units had to clear and mark gaps through their own minefields. Initially the mine removal party strove simply to locate the extent of the minefield and mark its boundaries, at least in the vicinity of the breach or gap that was to be cleared. Mines were then detected by visual indicators, magnetic mine detectors, or by the most common and effective means – probing. The easiest, quickest, and safest way to clear or breach a minefield was to detonate the individual mines with small demolition charges, which of course negated the booby-trapping threat. However, this method could not always be used owing to shortage of explosives, the potential for damage to nearby structures, or a wish not to alert the enemy. If demolitions could be used but were in short supply, only those mines found to be booby-trapped were exploded, rather than risking soldiers in attempts to disarm them. Recovered enemy mines were valuable, as they would often be re-used by the lifters in their own minefields.

HAND GRENADES

The US and UK employed scores of different types of antipersonnel, antitank, incendiary, white phosphorus, colored smoke, and other special types of hand

A major in the Royal Electrical & Mechanical Engineers (REME) gives SOE trainees instruction on sabotaging a locomotive, using a large-scale model. If the cylinder could be damaged with explosives then repairs would take months, but there were simpler methods that could be employed by patriotic railwaymen. Lubricating pipes could be simply hammered flat, or blocked by stuffing with rags; and introducing abrasive powder into lubricating oil or grease could cause wheel-axles to lock up when they got hot, often many miles from the site where the sabotage was committed. (IWM MH24439)

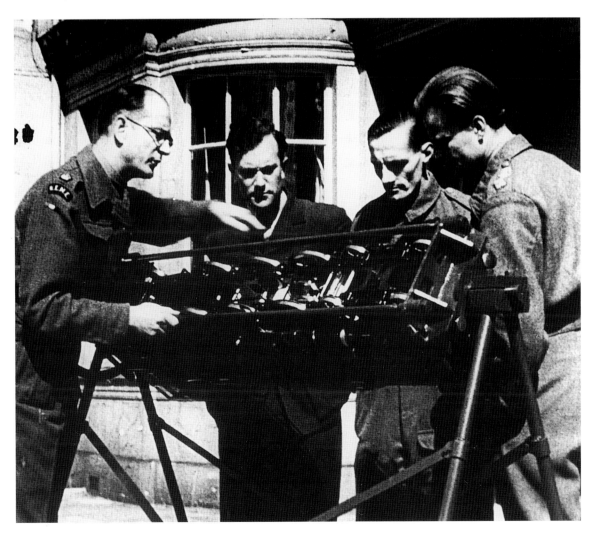

grenades, and with imagination most of these could be employed for sabotage or incorporated into booby traps in some manner. There were particular models, however, especially of British grenades, that were widely distributed to resistance groups in occupied countries.

The two most widely used Allied hand grenades were the US Mk II and Mk IIA1 defensive fragmentation grenades, commonly known as the "pineapple" or "frag grenade," and the British No.36M Mk I grenade or "Mills bomb." These were similar in design and function. Both had segmented cast-iron bodies; these segments were not for fragmentation effect, but provided a positive grip for wet or muddy hands – grenades usually shattered into many smaller fragments, although some times two or more of the segments would remain attached to one another. The Mills bomb held slightly more explosive than the US "pineapple." Both grenades had a "mousetrap"-type fuze. To use the grenade, an arming/safety pin was pulled

The most spectacular type of result gained by railroad sabotage: a locomotive derailed on the Grenoble–Marseilles line in southern France. Although it is sometimes assumed that the French Resistance did not become fully active until after the Allied landings in summer 1944, this was true only with regard to direct action, not in the case of industrial and railroad sabotage. Apart from cutting tracks, between June 1943 and May 1944 resisters sabotaged 1,822 locomotives, destroyed 2,500 freight cars and damaged 8,000 more. Given the Germans' strategic need to move troops and equipment back and forth between Western Europe and the Russian Front, this was a significant contribution. French railroad workers formed a Resistance group – the *Fer Réseau* (Iron Network) – to sabotage their own trains, and many were shot in German reprisals. (IWM MH11123)

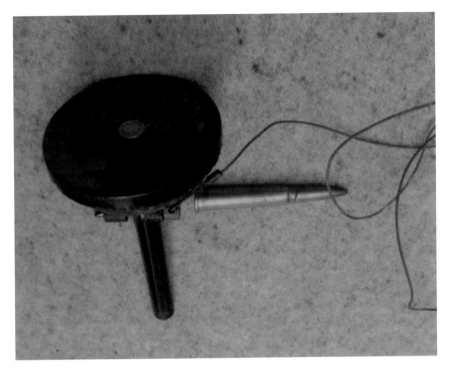

The British No.12 Mk I pressure-release switch was a 3in-diameter disc containing RDX/TNT. It was placed in a hole beneath a landmine, with the spike presumably resting on a solid base like a stone or piece of wood, and the disc flush with the bottom of the mine. A minimum of 2lb pressure was needed for safety. The arming pin was then pulled out with the cable, and the mine was camouflaged. (David Gordon Collection)

out by its ring with one hand while the fingers of the other hand held down a spring-loaded arming lever along the grenade's side. When the grenade was thrown the lever was released and flew off; this allowed a striker to snap down inside the grenade, where its firing pin struck a percussion cap. This immediately ignited a delay fuse to the detonator, of 4–5 seconds for the Mk II or 4 seconds for the No.36M (or 7 seconds, if it was fused to be fired

The conventional hand grenade provided the simplest pressure-release booby trap; here a US Mk II is placed beneath a discarded .50cal ammo can. Its weight holds down the arming lever, but here the pin has not yet been removed, nor the grenade camouflaged. A piece of ration-carton cardboard beneath the grenade helps prevent it settling into the earth if the cavity becomes wet.

PULL FUZE M1   PULL WIRE   STAKE

A US manual illustration of the simplest way to booby-trap a mine against lifting. An M1 pull-firing device is screwed into the secondary fuse well in the bottom of an M5 antitank mine and anchored to a stake; if the mine is lifted, the wire will be pulled and the mine will detonate. However, over time rainfall could cause earth to collapse into the hole, preventing a clean pull.

from a grenade-discharger). Either of these grenades could be rigged as a booby trap, either by anchoring it to a fixed object and attaching a tripwire or pull-cord to the arming ring, or by placing it under an object heavy enough to hold down the lever, and removing the pin; when the object was lifted the arming lever was released and the grenade armed. The problem with employing both these grenades for such purposes was that the delay fuse could not easily be removed and the detonator reattached; these were factory-installed and crimped in place, and their standard delay time somewhat reduced their effectiveness as booby traps.

The OSS went to great efforts to develop two impact-detonated fragmentation grenades, the T12 and T13. It was reasoned that any red-blooded American boy could throw a baseball with some degree of accuracy, and an effort began in late 1943 to develop a grenade the same size, weight, and shape as a baseball, designed to detonate upon impact. A complex impact fuze was adapted from the British No.274 "All Ways" type used on the No.69 ("Bakelite") and No.77 smoke grenades. Much difficulty was experienced in redesigning it so that it would project only minimally from the body, and the resultant T5-series fuze consisted of a convex, circular, knuckled arming cap ("butterfly cap") projecting slightly from the top. This was held in place by the thumb while the arming pin was pulled; when the grenade was thrown the cap flew off, a string attached to it pulled out a small, loosely-fitted arming pin, and the grenade detonated upon impact. Its minimum throwing range was 25ft to ensure that the fuze had time to arm in flight. As it was thought that it could be thrown at parked aircraft or moving vehicles, the OSS encouraged its development and used some on covert operations. The first version, the T12, weighed 5.5oz like a baseball, but was too light to be effective, and 825,000 of the subsequent 11.9oz T13 were ordered in early 1944. Nicknamed the "Beano," its development was too prolonged, and in any case conventional troops did not desire an impact grenade. Some T13s were used by paratroopers in the summer of 1944, with resulting casualties from premature detonations; there was also a high dud rate, and the project was dropped in June 1945.

Three types of specialized British grenades were widely supplied to resistance groups, and the first two were also used by the OSS and US paratroopers. The No.75 antitank grenade/mine was known as the "Hawkins"; actually a small landmine, it was introduced in mid-1942. This extremely versatile 2lb 4oz munition could be buried as a landmine (two side-by-side were recommended for use against tanks), thrown as an antitank grenade, or used as a demolition charge. The Hawkins grenade was fabricated from a 1-imperial-pint rectangular can. Two support brackets were welded to one side and a metal pressure plate fitted over these, covering two holders for chemical exploders; when the pressure plate was crushed the exploders were initiated, immediately igniting the detonators and explosive filler. The No.75 could be thrown in front of moving vehicles; five or six could be strung at 2ft intervals along a wire or cord "necklace" and pulled across a road in a vehicle's path; or they could be surreptitiously placed under the front and rear end of a parked tank's treads, to detonate when it moved.

When simply thrown on the ground they might land with the pressure plate up or down, but either way a vehicle's weight would detonate them; any that were not run over could be recovered and re-used. In the sabotage mode they could also be placed under a railroad tie as a pressure mine, or fastened to a rail with a delay fuze to cut it; several could also be linked with four wraps of cordtex to destroy a section of railroad track. For use as a grenade or demolition charge a friction igniter, a length of safety fuse, and a detonator were inserted in one of the exploder holders.

The 2.25lb No.82 antitank hand grenade or "Gammon bomb" was adopted in mid-1943. It consisted of a No.247 "All Ways" impact fuze

At a factory somewhere in Britain two workers pack No.74 grenades. The "sticky bombs" are already in their protective casings; the screw-on handles were packed around the sides of the box of five spherical heads. They will now be sent to an explosive-ordnance factory to be filled. (IWM D14775A)

An M1 pressure-release firing device fitted to a US Mk II grenade; this required at least 2lb weight on the activation lever to prevent it from detonating. (David Gordon Collection)

assembly fitted to a stockinette bag – actually a skirt, open at the bottom with an elasticated hem. As required for the task, a varied amount of "gelidnite," PE, slab guncotton, or ammonal was pressed into a ball and placed in the stockinette bag. For an antitank grenade a large amount was required; a smaller quantity of PE might be used for knocking out a machine-gun nest. Early versions had a 4.5in-long fly-off arming tape on the All Ways fuze rather than the normal 11.5in; the longer tape was adopted because of the danger posed by the short tape if the grenade was thrown at too short a range from the target.

The No.74 or ST ("sticky-type") antitank grenade was none too popular, for a number of reasons: it had the unpleasant habit of sticking to the uniforms of careless handlers, and was hazardous to use. It was developed in early 1940 as a sabotage weapon by the War Office Directorate of Military Intelligence's MD1 organization. Offered to the British Army, it was at first considered too dangerous; however, given the desperate need for antitank weapons after Dunkirk it was soon being issued. The "ST's" outer cover consisted of a two-piece, hinged, stamped metal sphere. Inside was a spherical glass flask filled with liquid explosive, and covered with stockinette material thickly coated with a very adhesive lime glue. A plastic throwing-handle screwed into the bottom of the flask, containing a fuse, detonator and priming-pellet assembly, and fitted with a spring-loaded metal arming lever held by a cotter pin.

To use the grenade, a retaining pin was first pulled out to allow the outer tin hemispheres to open and fall off, exposing the sticky surface. The safety pin through the handle was then pulled out, and the grenade was thrown from about 20 yards; the arming lever flew off, igniting the 5-second delay fuse. In theory the sticky coating stuck the explosive-filled flask to the side of the tank, where it detonated, relying on blast effect. It would not stick to a vertical or to a wet, muddy, or oily sloping surface, but it would certainly cling to a careless thrower's uniform. It was in fact recommended that instead of being thrown the No.74 should be hand-emplaced to an AFV's firing-port cover, or a pillbox door to unhinge it; in this case it had to be smashed against the target with enough force to break the flask, while releasing the arming lever with a sharp, positive movement, and the soldier then had to withdraw at least 10 yards before it detonated. The "ST" saw little action with the British, but it was provided to the French Resistance.

The Tank Destroyer School at Camp Hood, Texas, also developed an expedient "sticky grenade" of questionable effectiveness. It consisted of a GI sock filled with at least 2lb of TNT or PE, a 30-second time fuse, a No.8 detonator, with a throwing-stick inserted or a web throwing-sling attached. It was supposed to be dipped in a bucket of tar or covered with heavy axle grease, and slapped onto or thrown at a tank, to which it was hoped that it would cling (not likely, on a hot day.)

The little British general purpose or GP grenade could be used as a conventional high-explosive 1lb blast hand grenade, but was actually intended either as a sabotage device, or for any number of them to be bundled into a larger demolition charge. It was not issued to regular troops, but to SOE elements. It consisted of a thin metal rectangular case with a screw cap over the detonator well. The No.247 impact fuze could be fitted to the GP grenade to make it suitable for antipersonnel use (although it generated limited fragmentation), and against unarmored vehicles. As a demolition charge it could cut through ¾in of steel plate; two placed 1m apart, linked by detcord and tamped down, could cut railroad track.

The infamous British No.74 "sticky type" grenade, with the protective metal shell opened to expose the glue-soaked stockinette covering of the glass flask, which was filled with Nobel No.823 liquid explosive. The "ST" was withdrawn from service in 1943 due to the deterioration of the explosive filler, and the glue coating drying out in storage. A box of them was unearthed in France a few years ago, presumably buried by the *Maquis*; the stockinette and adhesive had dried out into a brittle, woody shell, but they were otherwise intact. (David Gordon Collection)

Captured Axis grenades were also widely used by resistance groups, and cached stocks of their own country's pre-war grenades were also sometimes available.

Incendiary devices

A large variety of small incendiary devices were widely used for sabotage, though thermite was the most common filler. They ranged in size from 3oz to several pounds, and came in a wide range of containers made of cardboard, fiberboard, Bakelite, tin, steel, magnesium (which burned), and cellulose acetate. Many incendiary charges were simply small containerized blocks of thermite or similar compounds ignited by some delay-fusing system or device.

Ignition systems included quickmatch, time-delay safety fuse, time pencils, grenade-like lever-activated fuzes, friction igniters, and percussion igniters (which had to be struck on a solid object). The use of incendiary devices was limited only by the imagination. Fire-starting compounds could cause far more damage than much larger amounts of explosives; besides destroying equipment, structures, and material, such incendiaries could be used to create diversions or confusion. However, to be effective they had to be placed in direct contact with the target or material to be ignited; flammable materials had to be in place to spread the flames, and the target itself or a significant portion of it had to be flammable. For example, simply placing an incendiary device among fuel drums might not be sufficient to ignite all of them. They usually needed an explosive charge to actually rupture and ignite them, and several such charges might have to be distributed throughout a large fuel dump to ensure that the blaze spread before it could be contained by firefighters.

A selection of such devices developed by the SOE and OSS are illustrated on Plate H. The US also used the AN-M14 incendiary grenade, a beercan-sized hand-emplaced thermite grenade. The British provided several such devices, ranging from the 2oz Mk I incendiary block (measuring 1¼in × 2½in × 5¼in), through 1¼lb and 1¾lb Mk II incendiary bombs, to the 2½lb Mk II thermite bomb – though despite its larger charge, this too measured only 3in × 5in. No such munitions were yet available in North Africa in autumn 1941, when the embryonic L Detachment, SAS, was in need of a hand-delivered incendiary bomb for attacking parked aircraft and fuel depots. The Australian Capt John S. "Jock" Lewes filled the need by developing a 1lb hand-thrown bomb made up of a PE slab rolled in motor oil and thermite powder, in a tin fitted with a time pencil. These "Lewes bombs" were also sometimes hidden in aircraft with a long-delay time pencil, to detonate days later or, hopefully, even in flight.

Early-warning devices

Units in defensive positions, day and night, needed a means to detect enemy troops infiltrating their lines or approaching on routes that could not be kept under surveillance from their positions. Outposts and listening posts could not cover every approach, especially in densely overgrown or extremely rough terrain. In some instances antipersonnel mines, booby-trapped hand grenades, and similarly rigged small demolition charges were emplaced on likely avenues; their detonation not only warned of the enemy's approach, but inflicted casualties and delay, and might even force them to withdraw once they had lost the element of surprise. Early-warning devices, like the obstacles they were emplaced in, needed to be covered by observation and fire to be useful; even if out of the direct line of fire of small arms, they could be covered with indirect machine gun and mortar fire.

The most basic means of early warning was simply to be familiar with the ground immediately in front of one's position. Which areas had bare or rocky ground that could be crossed quietly? Were there any dense brush, long grass, wet or muddy areas, or others covered with gravel or dead leaves that would be noisy to cross? Units had to occupy the ground before dark in order to study the terrain before them.

The simplest early-warning device was the rattle alarm dating back to World War I. This was a ration tin with a few pebbles or empty cartridge cases placed inside, hung up in a barbed-wire obstacle or simply on a tripwire, ideally within hand-grenade range of friendly positions. When the alarms were triggered the defenders would throw grenades so as not reveal their positions by firing small arms.

Trip flares were very effective in that they not only warned of the enemy's approach, but illuminated the area to allow them to be engaged, and might give the defenders an idea of the enemy's strength and deployment. A side benefit of this was that the sudden dazzling ignition of a flare not only scared the daylights out of the enemy, but blinded them and made it difficult to determine where defending small-arms fire came from. Most trip flares burned on the ground, but others launched a parachute-suspended flare into the air, to illuminate a larger area. They could be placed to warn of the enemy's approach at a distance beyond surveillance range, allowing pre-planned indirect fires to be placed in the area.

The US used three types of trip flares. The M48 parachute trip flare, available from 1943, was based on the M2A3 antipersonnel mine, a "Bounding Betty" type. It consisted of a 2.5in-diameter tube fixed to a base plate, beside which was a longer, narrow tube with the triggering device on top and containing the detonator system. When buried and lightly camouflaged it could be activated by stepping on one of three prongs, or by tripping a wire up to 80ft long. Anyone who stepped on it was hit by the bounding flare and became a casualty; the parachute-

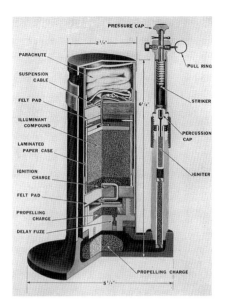

The US M48 parachute trip flare was based on the "bounding" antipersonnel mine, which fired an air-bursting 60mm mortar shell. It could be activated by pressure on the cap at top right, or by a tripwire. The 110,000-candlepower flare rose to heights between 250 and 400ft, and illuminated an area out to a 300yd radius for some 20 seconds while it drifted down.

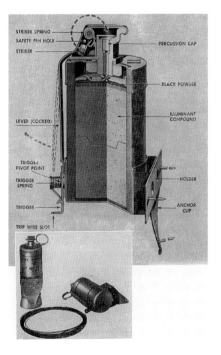

The US M49 surface trip flare could be nailed to a tree or stake, and was activated by tripwire. The 40,000-candlepower flare could light up a 300yd radius area for about one minute. Such early-warning devices were especially difficult to detect, being well hidden and usually encountered at night.

Two examples of rattle-trap early-warning devices, simply made by putting a few pebbles or old cartridge cases into an empty ration can and stringing it on a wire – note that the left-hand example has been smeared with mud to cut reflections. The cans were hooked on either by leaving the opened tops attached and bending them over the wire, or – more securely – by punching holes under the lip and wiring it to the obstacle. In wet weather holes were punched in the bottoms to prevent the cans from filling with water, which would muffle the rattle or could freeze; snow or clogging with fallen leaves could also silence them.

suspended 110,000-candlepower flare rose to between 250 and 400ft, and illuminated a 300yd-radius area with white-to-yellowish light for 20 seconds. The M49 surface trip flare, which came into use late in 1944, was a fiber canister containing the illuminate and fitted with a grenade-type lever-release instantaneous fuse. It had a mounting bracket and three nails to fasten it to a post or tree several inches off the ground, and a 45ft tripwire was attached to a spring-loaded trigger; when this was released it ignited the 40,000-candlepower yellowish flare, lighting up a 300yd radius for about a minute. The Navy developed the Mk 1 Mod 0 surface trip flare for the Marines, consisting of a steel tube with a pull-type firing device fitted on the upper side. It was fastened around a tree or stake with a supplied web strap, and 80ft of tripwire was provided; when tripped, a 75,000-candlepower yellow flare illuminated a 75yd radius for 65 seconds.

The "silent sentry" early-warning device was improvised in Italy to assist in night security, and could readily be made up in the field from standard-

E *"PLAN VERT"*: RAILROAD SABOTAGE, FRANCE, JUNE 1944

Railroad sabotage was one of the most frequent partisan activities in all theaters of war. Rail lines were difficult to guard effectively; they required only a small amount of explosive to cut; and the payoff was high, both in terms of damage to trains and in the delays caused. Immediately before the D-Day landings in Normandy the London-based SOE radioed coded orders for many waiting resistance groups to cut railroads (*Plan Vert*) in order to prevent German reinforcements reaching the invasion front. Only a small number of *maquisards* were necessary to emplace the pre-prepared charges, although ideally numerous groups would attack the lines through a particular area on the same night, and then conduct repeated follow-on attacks. A 1lb charge could cut a rail, but ideally several charges were set and linked by detcord to destroy a whole length of track, making it more difficult to repair. One man or woman would provide close-in protection, while others would be posted as lookouts further down the tracks in both directions and on their planned escape route. Preferably, they cut rail lines some distance from villages, in the (often vain) hope that the Germans would not carry out reprisals against innocent hostages. In fulfilment of *Plan Violet*, the resistance also cut adjacent telephone wires, dragging down lengthy sections.

issue materials; the M49 surface trip flare was not yet widely available, and this device served as a substitute. It was designed to fire two 37mm red, green, or amber Very flare cartridges in succession. Each was installed on a separate wooden stake, and they were fired by a tripwire that activated two M1 pull-firing devices. One set off the first flare, while the other ignited safety fuse leading to the second flare; the length of this fuse determining the interval between the ignition of the flares. Ideally, the time lag was long enough to allow an enemy patrol to recover from their initial shock and get back on their feet by the time the second flare fired. By gauging the direction of the first light, defending troops could prepare to fire in the right direction when the second flare illuminated the enemy.

Tangle-foot wire was another means of early warning; this was simply horizontal barbed wire tautly strung a foot or less off the ground, or in loose loops intended to catch intruder's feet. Tangle-foot could be strung between or forward of barbed wire barriers, to hamper the enemy infiltrators – an equipment-laden soldier tripping over at night can be noisy. Within urban areas, soldiers learned to listen at night for crunching footfalls treading on broken glass, bits of mortar and masonry, and splintered wood.

When a flare ignited, soldiers were taught to freeze in place and not move until it had burned out, then to move rapidly out of the area as quietly as possible. If they were engaged they were immediately to return fire; whether they attacked or withdrew depended on the tactical situation – as did the defenders' action. Often defenders would hold their fire rather than give away their positions, only opening fire if the intruders launched an attack.

(Of course, any of these alarms might equally well be triggered by animals, birds, hard rain, wind, and falling branches.)

DIRECT-ACTION TACTICS

The ambush and the raid were two key techniques employed by resistance fighters and partisans, and sabotage devices and booby traps could be employed during the execution of either of these.

The detailed and sophisticated ambush and raiding techniques developed since the 1950s during wars of insurgency and counterinsurgency did not exist during World War II; tactics were very basic, and groups developed their own preferred methods through trial and error. These were tailored to local conditions of terrain, weather, civilian activity, enemy tactics and capabilities, availability and types of weapons, and other factors. Partisans were adept at harassing actions, a form of economy-of-force tactics intended to keep the enemy off balance, create confusion and uncertainty, hamper rear-area activities, degrade morale, force the deployment of security forces that could otherwise be used at the front, and divert and expend resources.

Such actions might also reinforce the morale of the civilian population, but they could easily become counterproductive when the enemy undertook harsh reprisals against the innocent and helpless. They also needed careful timing; to coincide with the Normandy landings in June 1944, *Maquis* groups behind the front were ordered to carry out a program of road ambushes (*Plan Tortue*), usually orchestrated by Allied "Jedburgh" liaison teams and supported by heavily armed British SAS detachments or American OSS Operational Groups. While successes were achieved in areas that could expect rapid liberation by the Allied armies, three premature all-out confrontations

with German forces launched at their own initiative by thousands of *maquisards* deeper inside the country resulted in defeats and very high losses.

Ambushes

An ambush is a surprise attack from a position against a moving enemy force. Ambushes might take place on a forest path or mountain trail, a country road, a city street, a railroad track or a barge canal – any place the enemy might travel on foot or by vehicles. Booby traps and sabotage devices might be incorporated into an ambush – set on the route, to initiate the ambush, or left behind among bodies and damaged vehicles, to inflict casualties among a relief force.

The basic idea of an ambush is to achieve complete surprise, destroy or drive away the enemy, capture and/or destroy material, and withdraw safely. Ambushes need to have a specific object: to target particular individuals, or to harass, kill or capture personnel; to destroy equipment, and capture weapons and supplies; to disrupt or delay enemy movements and actions; and, always, to create confusion and degrade enemy morale. Partisan ambushes on convoys had the triple benefits of destroying transport, denying supplies to the enemy, and capturing supplies for the partisans' own use.

An ambush could be launched against any size of force the ambushers felt capable of tackling; even a small party might attack a larger force simply as a hit-and-run harassing attack. The size of the ambush party depended on the strength of the column to be ambushed and its escorting force and armament, its size and length (number of vehicles, length of train, etc), the terrain, and the exact object of the ambush. Repeated small-scale

SS-Obergruppenführer Reinhard Heydrich's Mercedes 320 convertible after the ambush in Prague on May 27, 1942. The damage caused by Jan Kubis' thrown Hawkins grenade is evident, though not dramatic. It was enough, however: Heydrich's deep fragment wounds, and the horsehair seat-stuffing driven into his internal organs, killed him from septicemia a week later. (IWM HU47379) ambushes executed by handfuls of men against "easy" targets such as small groups of soldiers or one or two vehicles proved very effective in wearing down enemy morale.

The most important aspect of the ambush force, regardless of its strength, was its organization and assignment of responsibilities – there is much more to an ambush than simply lining everyone up along a road, and opening fire on signal. An attack group was specified, and each man was assigned a sector of fire, to ensure that no part of the "kill zone" was left uncovered. Teams had to be assigned to knock out the lead and tail vehicles, as well as combat or security vehicles. An assault or recovery group might also be designated, to enter the kill zone to destroy vehicles, take prisoners, finish off the wounded (partisan warfare was vicious), and recover weapons, equipment and supplies; specific individuals might be designated to recover documents, other special items, or prisoners. Ideally there would be an overall ambush commander responsible for all aspects of the operation, as well as an attack group commander concerned only with the main attack on the target.

Security was critical, and several security teams might be formed. One would be placed on either flank to provide early warning of the target's approach, to protect the flanks of the ambush party, and to engage enemy fleeing from the kill zone. At least one security team was necessary to secure the ambush party's rear, and others might be employed to watch other routes leading into the area. As the ambush force withdrew, these teams would protect its withdrawal.

A successful ambush depended upon surprise and firepower. Simultaneous and immediate opening of fire was essential to overwhelm and neutralize the enemy; this fire could not be reduced until the enemy was destroyed or withdrew, especially since the ambush force was usually smaller than the enemy force. As little time as possible was spent at the ambush site. The withdrawal had to be rapid and orderly, and the partisans would quickly disperse and hide their weapons and any loot.

One famous example of a tightly focused and successful ambush – although at dreadful cost – was the attack on SS-Obergruppenführer Reinhard Heydrich in Prague, Czechoslovakia, in May 1942, when hand-picked Czech agents trained by the SOE were parachuted in with the specific mission of assassinating him. General Heydrich, the Reichsprotektor of Bohemia and Moravia and second only to Heinrich Himmler in the SS hierarchy, was the symbol of the Nazi occupation. He was also so arrogantly sure of his domination over the Czech people that he travelled between his country home and his Prague offices by a regular route, alone but for his driver in an unescorted Mercedes touring car. On May 27, two volunteers waited at a suburban site where the road made a hairpin turn that forced the open-topped car to slow to about 12mph. At the critical moment Josef Gabcik's Sten gun jammed, but Jan Kubis threw an early example of the No.75 "Hawkins" grenade which detonated against the car's side. The badly wounded Heydrich leapt out and attempted to pursue (it is debatable whether or not he actually fired his pistol), but he soon collapsed. His wound proved mortal, and he died on June 6. By June 20 – when the attackers and their back-up party were cornered in the Karl Borromeus Church, and shot themselves after a long, fierce defense of the crypt – mass arrests and reprisals had already been carried out. In total it is estimated that up to 5,000 men, women and children were murdered in revenge for Heydrich's assassination

August 1944: in the streets of Paris, a French Resistance fighter armed with an SOE-supplied 9mm Sten Mk II sub-machine gun is photographed along with a US Army lieutenant. Watching in the background, unimpressed, are a couple of metropolitan policemen; not long beforehand, they might as easily have been pursuing the *résistants* as supporting them. (ARC 531322)

– most notoriously, the population of the small village of Lidice, near Kladno, which was surrounded by Security Police on June 9. Next day 199 men and boys were shot, 195 women were shipped off to Ravensbrück concentration camp, and 90 children were deported elsewhere. At least another 1,330 Czech civilians were executed by military courts; of 500 Berlin Jews arrested on May 29, 150 were executed by June 6; and by June 12 trains had taken some 3,000 Czech Jews from the Theresienstadt ghetto eastwards to extermination camps.

This was only one of the best-known instances of the Nazis' policy of mass reprisals against civilians in occupied Europe – a practice that naturally discouraged many resistance groups from taking the usually pointless risks of direct action until the Allied landings and advances of 1944 made it

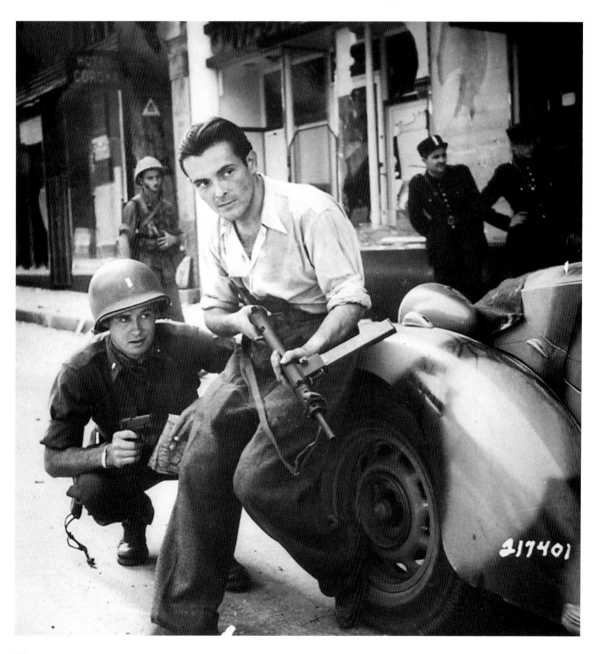

feasible. (Even so, it is estimated that in occupied France alone the Germans executed at least 70,000 Resistance members and hostages; a typical ratio was 50 hostages shot for each German killed.)

Raids

A raid is a surprise attack usually on a fixed objective, characterized by rapid, violent action followed almost at once by withdrawal – there is no intention of occupying the objective for any longer than necessary to accomplish the mission. As opposed to an ambush party, the raiding force usually had to be larger than the defending force in order to overwhelm it quickly, accomplish their mission, and fight their way out. Nevertheless, there were instances in which smaller raiding parties succeeded in neutralizing the enemy and accomplishing their mission; this required complete surprise, a superior plan and tactics, excellent control of forces and support, and the effective use of diversions. A raid might be conducted to destroy a critical facility or capability, to capture weapons, supplies, intelligence materials or key individuals, or to liberate prisoners. Whatever the primary goal, the aim would also be to kill as many of the enemy as possible and destroy their facilities and equipment.

Again, the organization of the raiding force was critical. The assault party might have to be broken down into groups and teams to attack or occupy particular objectives within the target area, and to accomplish specific tasks. Not all the raiders might be required to enter the target area – in most cases,

Across vast areas of only partly and temporarily occupied territory in the Soviet Union, villagers often had little choice over whether or not to take up arms. Preyed upon by the German occupiers and the Soviet partisans alike, they took to the forests when their communities were destroyed. This mother and son team are posed as if about to plant explosives on a railroad line, having carried the demolition charges in a burlap bag. (Nik Cornish Collection) the fewer the better, so as to maintain control, prevent confusion and friendly-fire casualties, and to manage a more organized withdrawal. Security teams were just as essential as they were for ambushes, in order to secure any approach routes that enemy reinforcements might use, warn of and delay such reinforcements, and cover the assault party's withdrawal.

Another important element of the raid was the support force, comprising riflemen and the crews of any machine guns and mortars, to place suppressive fire on the objective and any adjacent targets they might be assigned. It was essential that their fires were tightly controlled, ceasing or shifting to other targets when the assault party launched its attack. The supporting weapons might then be repositioned to engage any approaching enemy, or to cover the assault party's withdrawal; sometimes, however, it was better to withdraw the heavy weapons early, since they were slower to move.

Most raids by partisans were on a small scale and relatively simple in plan and organization, owing to their limited military experience, training, and discipline. Booby traps were sometimes left behind, but there was usually little time available to set them before the raiders had to withdraw.

Harassing actions

Harassment of the enemy was a main goal of partisans and saboteurs, and a role in which they were quite adept. While small-scale ambushes and raids come under this heading, booby traps and sabotage devices were also ideal for such purposes. The ultimate goals were, as always, to keep the enemy off balance and wear down his morale, to force him to commit men to escort and guard convoys and facilities, and to remind both the occupied civilian

 USE OF EXPLOSIVES FOR SABOTAGE

1: Explosive coal. SOE put some effort into developing explosive charges made to look like lumps of coal (the concept of the "coal torpedo" had in fact been developed by the Confederacy during the American Civil War.) These consisted of a cast shell that separated into two halves, each with a small hole in which an igniter match, short delay fuse, and a blasting cap were inserted prior to use. The color of coal varied greatly by region, from brown to deep black, so a small "coal camouflage kit" was provided to enable agents to match the charge to local colors; this contained paints, thinner, putty plugs, brushes, and spatula, but it took a good eye to make the coal look natural. Bulk coal stocks were seldom guarded, and the explosive lumps would be tossed into coal tenders and trucks, dumps, and bins. With any luck the booby-trapped coal might be shoveled into a boiler firebox on a locomotive or ship, or into a factory furnace; it would not blow up the boiler, but would damage the firebox and hopefully the water tubes. Similar chunks of explosive-filled wood were also provided.

2: Explosive rat. Dead rats filled with PE were prepared by taxidermists; they incorporated a Mk II 1oz guncotton primer, a short length of time fuse, and a No.10 time pencil. The idea was that a dead rat left near a boiler or furnace might be shoveled into it for disposal. In that case no activation of the delay fusing was necessary, but it could also be activated and left where it would inflict damage.

3: Explosive oiler. There was also an explosive-filled railroad engineer's oiler can. In the middle of the PE charge was a cavity containing actual oil around the primer and time pencil, allowing some to be poured out to satisfy inspectors or even to fool the locomotive crew. The spout was removed to activate the time pencil, and refitted. If activated and left aboard a German-manned locomotive, its detonation would disable the crew in the confined cab.

4: Tin can grenade. SOE and OSS agents parachuted in to assist resistance groups taught them how to make simple grenades using tins filled with a few ounces of PE, and fitted with a blasting cap and a very short time fuse. Nails and gravel could be pressed into the PE for fragmentation. Larger tins could be used, but their throwing range was reduced.

5: Molded PE. The most basic munition of all – a molded ball of plastic explosive with a knotted length of detcord embedded in it. "Pearl necklaces" made in this way and fitted with time pencils were handy for bringing down telegraph poles.

6a–6e: Attachment of blasting caps and fuse. These examples show how blasting caps, time-delay safety fuse, and detcord were attached to US and British fuse adapters. **(6a)** US firing device adapter; **(6b)** US firing device adapter with aluminum No.8 blasting cap crimped on; **(6c)** British fuse adapter with safety fuse inserted; **(6d)** British fuse adapter with copper blasting cap inserted and cordtex beside it; and **(6e),** the same, after wrapping with cloth friction tape.

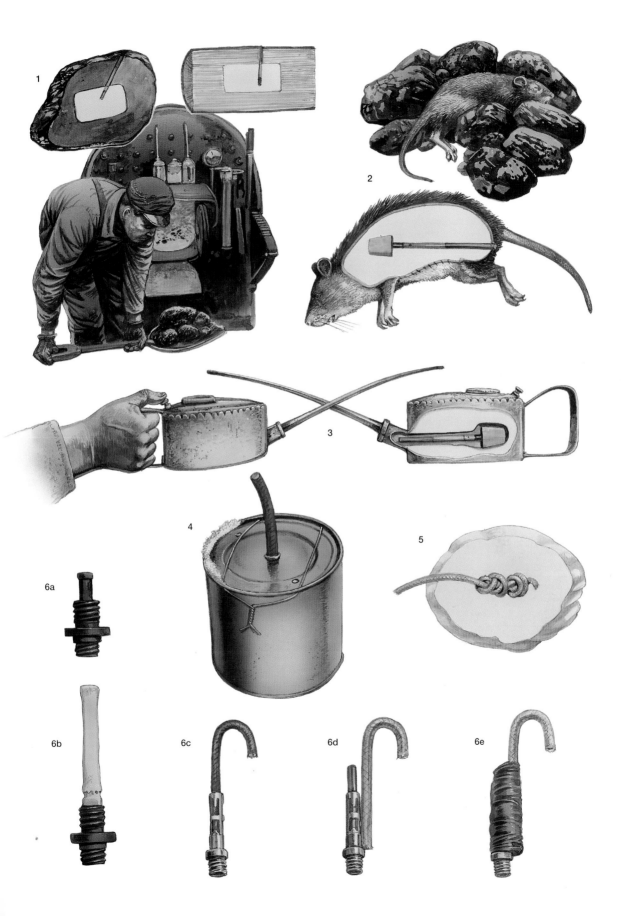

population and the enemy of the latter's vulnerabilities. Indirect harassing actions could also improve the morale and will to resist of the repressed population, while minimizing the risk of the occupiers shooting hostages in reprisal. In this regard the ideal was "invisible destruction" – incidents where damage appeared to be due to naturally occurring equipment malfunctions, breakage, and wear and tear. More usually the responsibility of saboteurs was obvious, but the acts were not significant enough to justify major efforts to track down the culprits. Nevertheless, the cumulative damage inflicted might be considerable, and the whole contributed to the war effort.

Harassment ran the gamut from painting protest slogans on walls, spreading propaganda leaflets, damaging vehicles and machinery, cutting telephone and power lines, disrupting utilities and services, mining roads and placing booby traps, and so on (hopefully) *ad nauseam*. The Germans obliged many businesses and factories in occupied countries to shift to manufacturing war materials, producing food for the occupation forces, or providing a wide range of other services. Workers and managers could accomplish much in the way of work slowdowns, deliberately poor production techniques and workmanship, use of inferior materials, lost paperwork, late delivery, or misdirected shipments of materials and components. More directly, sniper attacks on convoys, individual vehicles, troop columns, facilities and installations could be very disruptive, as could random drive-by attacks and selective assassinations – both by gunfire, and by grenades, explosive charges, or incendiaries.

COUNTER-SABOTAGE

The Nazis conducted a relentless campaign of counterespionage and counterinsurgency in their efforts to apprehend Allied agents and local activists, and to suppress any form of direct or indirect resistance. Despite its utter ruthlessness, however, the Nazi state machinery devoted to these tasks was so complex that its efficiency actually suffered from the turf wars between parallel organizations.[6]

Counterespionage, countersabotage and counterinsurgency, strictly defined, are quite different activities, but the German apparatus for all three converged at its upper echelons. At the apex of the whole Nazi police state, Heinrich Himmler was simultaneously the Reichsführer-SS (National Leader of the SS), and the Chef der Deutschen Polizei (Chief of German Police) within the Interior Ministry. Himmler controlled both the Hauptamt der Ordnungspolizei (Head Office of the Order Police, OrPo), administering the multifarious branches of the uniformed national police, under the leadership of Gen Kurt Daluege; and the Reichssicherheitshauptamt (Head Office for National Security, RSHA) – headed initially by Gen Heydrich, and from January 1943 by Gen Ernst Kaltenbrunner – which controlled the Security Police (SiPo).

The SiPo was in fact a blanket term, embracing three services, of which many personnel had been recruited among politically reliable members of the conventional police forces. The senior was the Security Service (SD – the

---

6 For material on the interpenetration of the Nazi Party, SS and German government hierarchies, and on the various police and security organizations, see Elite 157: *The German Home Front 1939–45*; Warrior 61: *German Security and Police Soldier 1939–45*; and Men-at-Arms 434: *World War II German Police Units.*

France, 1940: an NCO of the German Army Feld-gendarmerie, instantly recognizable by his metal gorget plate, checks the overloaded truck of a refugee family. (Robert Noss Collection)

SS intelligence and counterintelligence branch), which was a uniformed organization. The agents of the Secret State Police (Gestapo), and the detectives of the National Criminal Police (KriPo) who were subordinate to them, normally operated in plain clothes. In general terms, no part of this apparatus was subject to judicial oversight, and it wielded the power of life and death simply by administrative orders. In investigating cases of sabotage, treason, and very widely-defined "criminal" activity against the State or the Party, both at home and in occupied territories, the SD and Gestapo enjoyed a completely free hand. *The Nacht und Nebel* ("Night and Fog") Decree, enacted on December 7, 1941, was an instrument of terror that essentially allowed the arrest, interrogation under torture, execution, or despatch to a concentration camp of any person, German or foreign, without any due process of law or any public announcement – its victims simply disappeared.

There was a good deal of overlapping and friction between the different branches even within the police and security apparatus – and particularly, in occupied territories, between the RSHA and the parallel military intelligence and security organization which answered to the Defense Forces High Command (OKW): the Abwehr (military intelligence department, headed by Adm Wilhelm Canaris), with its Geheime Feldpolizei (GFP). This Secret Field Police was the German Army's counterespionage, countersabotage, and counterpropaganda agency, and was also responsible for detection of treasonable activity, VIP escort, prisoner-of-war interrogation, and related activities. The long campaign by the SS to take control of the Abwehr succeeded in February 1944, after which date the military intelligence apparatus was swallowed by the RSHA. The Army's conventional Feldgendarmerie or Military Police branch provided law-enforcement, checkpoint and traffic-control duties within 12 miles of the front lines, but they also assisted occupation authorities behind the lines, and collected and escorted POWs.

The complex details of organization and prerogatives differed between the occupied territories; however, in the West the most important of the various resources available to the commander of the military occupation authorities (Militärbefehlshaber) and the regional Higher SS and Police Leader (Höhere SS und Polizei Führer) was actually the occupied country's own national and municipal police. These operated under the oversight and direction of quite small numbers of SD and Gestapo personnel, whose task was aided by a depressingly widespread practice of informing and anonymous denunciation by civilians. In France, for example, any resistance was in direct violation of the armistice signed by the Vichy regime: "The French Government will forbid French citizens to fight against Germany in the service of states with which the German Reich is still at war. French citizens who violate this provision are to be treated by German troops as insurgents." French government authorities actively employed the national police (Police Nationale), national militarized police (Gendarmerie Nationale), and, from its raising in January 1943, a Vichy paramilitary militia (Milice française), against any form of dissent and resistance – indeed, the blue-uniformed *miliciens* were considered by many to be more brutal than most Germans.

The Germans used the term *Banditen* ("bandits") for all resistance fighters throughout the occupied territories. On August 23, 1942 the Army High Command issued a directive that for psychological reasons this pejorative term was to be used in preference to "partisan"; it implied that resisters were not entitled to the protections of the Geneva Convention, and could properly be interrogated and executed without mercy. Other terms in use included *bewaffnite Bander* (armed gangs), *Bolshevik aufwieglers* (Bolshevik agitators),

G   GERMAN DETECTION EFFORTS

The Germans used common methods of searching for and detecting mines.

1: Magnetic mine detectors such as this *Wein 41 Minensuchgerät* (Vienna 1941 mine searching equipment), operated by a Pionier, saw only limited use.

2: The *Minensuchstab 39 (Ms.39)*, literally "mine-searching rod," or *Sucheisen n.A.* ("searching iron, new type") consisted of a 2ft light alloy tube with a thin steel point; a 3ft extension could be fitted to allow the searcher to stand. When the probing point struck a hard object such as a mine, the hollow alloy tube generated a vibrating effect to alert the user. A simpler 5ft pointed steel rod was also used, as was an awkward 15ft rack-like device with tines similar to a hayfork. Bayonets – either handheld or fixed to a rifle – and sharpened wooden sticks were also used to probe for mines. **3:** Lanes cleared through minefields were supposed to be 2m wide for infantry, 5m for one vehicle lane, and 10m for two-way traffic. These were marked with white or colored tape, the colors used to guide different units. The Germans marked booby-trapped areas with black-and-white signs, bearing an Iron Cross symbol or a death's-head.

4: In their efforts to combat the resistance groups in occupied territory, the Feldgendarmerie (Military Police), Geheime Feld Polizei (Secret Field Police), and local national police under Gestapo control established checkpoints and roadblocks, made security patrols, searched the transport networks, and followed up on informers' reports. Here a Feldgendarmerie NCO behind the front lines calls over a civilian to check his papers and search him. The unlucky patriot happens to be a *maquisard*, carrying an SOE-supplied suitcase containing two hidden incendiary charges. To open it safely, the right hand latch had to be pressed first, and held to the right while the left latch was opened; if not, the charges would ignite and destroy the contents of the case.

The Warsaw Ghetto, 1943: if it was alarming enough to be questioned by a Feld-gendarmerie "chained-dog," the Sicherheitsdienst had the instant power of life and death. Grey Allgemeine-SS open-collar or field-grey Waffen-SS closed-collar tunics, with a blank right collar patch and the "SD" left sleeve diamond, were also sometimes worn by other SiPo personnel, with a mix of SS and Police insignia. This makes exact identification from black-and-white photographs problematic. (USHMM)

Saboteure (saboteurs), and *Soldaten in zivilkleidung* (soldiers in civilian clothes). On October 18, 1942 Hitler even issued the infamous *Kommandobefehl* ("Commando Order"), which extended this treatment to uniformed Allied troops captured during behind-the-lines raids. This directive, removing the distinction between *Bandenkampf* and some conventional operations, shocked many Wehrmacht commanders, who ignored it where possible – but others did not.

For large-scale field operations against resistance and partisan groups, from the outbreak of war rifle battalions of the Schutzpolizei (Protection Police, SchuPo – the main executive branch of the OrPo) were raised to operate behind the front lines in the occupied territories, and their numbers expanded steadily. Since the SS and Police command structure was unified at national and regional level both inside and outside the Reich, the distinction between the two organizations became ever more blurred, and in 1943 the Police combat units were absorbed by the SS altogether. Starting in 1940, the Army also formed 15 second-line Security Divisions for antipartisan operations; all but one served in the East, but 325. Sicherungs-Division was headquartered in Paris in 1943–44. Apart from poor-quality German units, by 1944 about 70 Ostbataillonen – Wehrmacht units enlisted in the USSR, many of them from ethnic minorities – had been posted to Italy and France, and such troops were employed both in the front lines and for security duties. In the occupied Eastern Territories the Germans also formed many security and antipartisan units from locals. Typically these were recruited from among prewar pro-Fascist parties, from ethnic groups that felt themselves to be disenfranchised by former national governments, or simply from opportunist thugs. Such units were termed, e.g., Schutzmannschaft (security units) or Hilfspolizei (auxiliary police).

Detection and neutralization

In any of a wide range of specific environments – whether he was a *Landser* in the combat zone, a sentry at a rear-area installation, or a GFP Inspektor – a German's principal protection from booby traps and sabotage devices was constant and alert vigilance.

The detection of landmines, booby traps, and early-warning devices was not part of the soldiers' basic training, but they learned from practical experience and instruction at unit level. Well-worn footpaths were especially dangerous, and soldiers were taught to walk off to the sides; the enemy sometimes countered this by laying antipersonnel mines adjacent to trails, especially in light brush and weeds. Magnetic mine detectors were available to pioneers (combat engineers), but they were relatively scarce. They were also fairly heavy, used a great many batteries, required rotation of operators owing to the continuous buzzing tone in the earphones, and obliged the operator to walk upright through a minefield. Purpose-made mine probes were issued, but more use was made of homemade wooden probes, stiff wire, and bayonets. This apparently crude method was important, since the Red Army made widespread use of wooden mines containing only a few tiny metal parts indetectable by magnetic mine detectors. Magnetic mine detectors also confused operators by reacting to scrap metal such as discarded tin cans and shell fragments; sometimes the enemy would intentionally sow minefields with such scrap to hamper mine detectors and slow the clearance effort.

The Germans marked enemy minefields using signs inscribed with *Minen* (Mines), "*M*," or "*Mi*," as well as symbols such as a skull, crossed bones or both, or a raised hand indicating "Halt." These might be painted on black or white signboards, or on a central horizontal white band between contrasting upper and lower bands. Similar markings might be placed on a treetrunk or

Part of the contents of a container of weapons, ammunition and sabotage equipment, as parachuted to the French Resistance by the RAF. Containers usually had mixed contents, so that if one or more of the 12–18 containers in a single drop went astray, at least some of the requested items might be recovered. Typical loads might include 40 No.36 and 12 No.82 grenades, and 145lb/70kg of explosives. In this photo can be seen a dozen semiautomatic pistols of various makes, with ammunition; a large wrench for loosening rails (center), below sticks of plastic explosive; coils of fuse; No.36 grenades (top left), and (right of them) tins of detonators. These blasting caps were always packed separately, in small numbers in clearly marked tin or plastic canisters, and needed cautious handling. Despite their small size, they could cause serious injuries if they detonated in the hand. (IWM R354)

stump with a patch of bark shaved off, on large rocks, or on a building wall. Gaps and lanes were indicated by a signboard on one side of the opening, painted half white and half red or black; *Minen* might or might not be painted on the red or black end, and *Gasse* ("gap") or *entmint* ("removed") on the white end adjacent to the gap. Booby-trapped areas might be marked with signs bearing a death's-head or a Maltese cross. If minefields were discovered but could not be cleared, German forces might string a single knee-high wire or barbed-wire cattle fence, and set empty mine crates or simply stakes to warn the unwary.

Booby traps were more problematical; they were usually well concealed, no two might be alike, and there were no devices available to detect them. As in any other army, German troops were taught to be especially vigilant when entering facilities and areas recently occupied by the enemy. They were warned not to pick up or disturb desirable items such as weapons, munitions, food containers, or other small equipment. They had to be cautious opening doors and gates; it was better to enter and exit buildings through windows, but even these might be booby-trapped. Abandoned vehicles, especially AFVs – which would have to be inspected – were sometimes booby-trapped to make it dangerous to enter them, turn on the engines or move them.

Discovered booby traps might be blown in place, but it was often necessary to disarm them to prevent damage to buildings and facilities. Troops disarming booby traps would roll up their sleeves to prevent snagging on wires, and remove headgear so that their vision would not be restricted and to prevent a helmet from falling on or bumping into something dangerous. While most firing devices, mine fuzes, and booby-trapped grenades could be disarmed by reinserting arming pins, this was not always the safest method, since any jiggling might release the firing pin. If there was any difficulty inserting the pin, it should not be forced. Unscrewing a firing device from the charge could also activate it. If there was an exposed safety

---

H **INCENDIARY DEVICES**

Incendiary devices had the advantage of being both compact and capable of initiating a considerable amount of damage. If a fire took hold fast enough and got out of control before the fire services could respond, a hand-sized incendiary device had the potential to cause more damage than even hundreds of pounds of high explosive. Such devices could be used to create a diversion by causing confusion, to ignite fires among flammable structures or materials, and even to melt through metal to destroy equipment, damage electrical systems, etc.

1: US "M1 pocket incendiary." This was a 5½in × 3in × 1in celluloid case filled with jellied gasoline, with clips on both sides for time pencils.

2: British "large thermite well." The 7½in × 3¾in × 2in ceramic container with a steel base was covered with pasteboard, and filled with thermite. Beneath a pop-off cap, it was fitted with two lengths of safety fuse and two friction pull-igniters. It could melt through ¾in of casing steel.

3: British "small thermite well." Measuring 4½in × 3¼in × 1¾in, this smaller version lacked the steel base and had only one delay fuse and friction igniter. It was ideal for igniting fuel drums, and could be set up higher on the drum's side by using piled earth or gravel.

4: US "Firefly." This incendiary-explosive device could be hidden in the palm of the hand; its head was filled with TNT and lined with flammable magnesium. The pin was pulled and the device was dropped into a vehicle or aircraft fuel tank or a fuel drum. Swelling rubber discs released the firing pin after 2–5 hours – the colder the fuel, the longer the delay.

5: "Incendiary packet." This 3¼in × 6in × 1in tin box contained three matchbox-like cartons. One was filled with powdered sugar, one with potassium chlorate, and the third with five each green plastic ampoules of sulfuric acid for 2–4 hours' delay, and tan ampoules for 1–3 hours. Equal amounts of sugar and potassium chlorate were mixed in any handy container; two or more ampoules were activated by crushing, and left in the mixture, to ignite any flammable material. The packet held sufficient materials for five incendiary operations.

6: "Capsules H." These plastic capsules, ⅝in × ¼in, were issued 150 in a metal box. Two or more would be placed in a bottle of gasoline, kerosene, or any other flammable liquid, together with a few ounces of sulfuric acid (the acid was not provided; the saboteur was expected to obtain it locally from vehicle batteries.) The bottle was placed stopper-down against a suitable target; the acid and the capsules settled in the neck, and would ignite after about two hours.

This is a Red Army soldier, but the basic method of mine detection was the same for all armies: probing suspicious ground with a metal rod, spike or blade, here fixed to a wooden pole. One training method employed by the Germans on the Eastern Front was for experienced NCOs to lead a group of replacements to a Soviet minefield, where they would point out how to identify mine locations; they would then lead the men in walking through the minefield, identifying and marking mines. Pioneers became adept at spotting disturbed ground and ground-covering, shallow depressions of settled earth, small mounds in windblown sand or snow, dark patches in the soil, or cracks in frosty ground under thin snow. (Nik Cornish Collection)

fuse or detcord it was safest simply to cut it. The absolutely safest method, if the situation permitted, was to blow the charge with a 100g boring cartridge or a 200g charge – but of course this was not always possible, as its detonation might achieve the result sought by the saboteur.

Personnel responsible for the security of factories, facilities, and installations had perhaps the most difficult task. It was relatively easy for the resistance to smuggle in sabotage materials concealed on the person, in lunch pails or parcels, in material shipments, and so on. There were a great many hiding places, and with many people moving about it was comparatively easy to emplace an incendiary device, introduce damaging materials to machinery, or simply break something important. However, the certainty of reprisals for any damage that would be discovered on the spot limited what could be done by local workers or imported slave laborers alike. (There were instances when French railroad workers poured hydrochloric acid and nitric acid on German food supplies in freight cars, and hundreds were executed in retaliation.)

CONCLUSION

There is little information available to allow us to assess just how effective OSS- and SOE-supplied sabotage devices were, any more than devices fabricated locally by resistance groups. What few reports are available are in some instances inflated, while German reports tended to gloss over and minimize the damage – if it was even reported at all to higher authority. That does not mean that reprisals were not inflicted; indeed, there seem to have been many instances when the results of natural accidents, malfunctions, poor-grade materials, or simple human error were attributed to sabotage.

A great deal of effort and imagination went into the development of these devices at only a comparatively modest cost. Many were never distributed, and a proportion of those that were delivered were never used (some of these found an eventual use during the Cold War, which saw the introduction of similar but improved devices.)

The Allies' battlefield booby-trapping was rather limited owing to their being largely on the offensive. The widest use of booby traps was by British forces in North Africa, and this was mainly limited to antilifting devices in the extensive desert minefields. In any theater there were occasions when Allied forces were in the defense during pauses in the offensive, or when they conducted local withdrawals, and in those cases booby traps might be sown, usually in abandoned positions. Early-warning devices saw wide use, even during single-night halts, and some booby traps might be emplaced at the same time; the drawback was that time had to be taken to deactivate and recover them before the unit could move out – they could not be left behind, to endanger follow-on units that might occupy the same positions.

No statistical estimates are available of the numbers of casualties caused by Allied booby traps; the numbers were undoubtedly low, but it must be remembered that the main goal of booby-trapping was simply to damage the enemy's morale, to delay and otherwise hamper him.

RECOMMENDED READING

Brunner, John W., *OSS Weapons* (privately published, 1994)

Bull, Stephen (ed.), *Special Ops, 1939–1945: A Manual of Covert Warfare and Training* (Minneapolis, MN; Zenith Press, 2009)

Dear, Ian, *Sabotage & Subversion: Stories from the Files of the SOE and OSS* (London; Arms & Amour Press, 1996)

Jones, Ian, *Malice Aforethought: A History of Booby Traps from World War One to Vietnam* (London; Greenhill Books, 2004)

Lorain, Pierre, *Clandestine Operations: The Arms and Techniques of the Resistance, 1941–1944* (New York; Macmillan Publishing, 1972)

Melton, H. Keith, *OSS Special Weapons and Equipment: Spy Devices of WW II* (New York; Sterling Publishing, 1992 – r/p 1944 OSS Weapons catalog)

Seaman, Mark, *Secret Agent's Handbook of Special Devices* (Guilford, CT; Lyons Press, 2001 – r/ps 1942 & 1944 SOE catalogs)

West, Nigel, *Secret War: The True Story of SOE, Britain's Wartime Sabotage Organization* (London; Hodden & Stoughton, 1992)

OSS Sabotage and Demolition Manual (Boulder, CO; Paladin Press, 1973 – r/p of wartime manual)

Landmines and Booby Traps, FM 5-31 (November 1943, with 18 Changes to May 1945)

Landmines, TM 9-1940 (July 1943 with Change 1, August 1944)

British Demolition Stores, TM 9-1985-1 (July 1952)

(The above manuals are available from www.military-info.com.)

Mines and Booby Traps, Military Training Pamphlet No. 40 (May 1943)

Grenade, Small Arms Training Vol 1, Pamphlet 13 (War Office, July 1942)

INDEX

Note that references in **bold** are to plates and illustrations